THE FINDING
OF THE 'THIRD EYE'

The present volume is one of a sequence of books by the same author on the application of the Ancient Wisdom to modern living:

THE FINDING
OF THE 'THIRD EYE'

Vera Stanley Alder

Illustrations by the author

RIDER
London Melbourne Sydney Auckland Johannesburg

Rider & Company

An imprint of the Hutchinson Publishing Group

17–21 Conway Street, London W1P 6JD

Hutchinson Group (Australia) Pty Ltd
30–32 Cremorne Street, Richmond South, Victoria 3121
PO Box 151, Broadway, New South Wales 2007

Hutchinson Group (NZ) Ltd
32–34 View Road, PO Box 40-086, Glenfield, Auckland 10

Hutchinson Group (SA) Pty Ltd
PO Box 337, Bergvlei 2012, South Africa

First published 1938
Sixteenth impression 1967
This edition 1982

© Vera Stanley Alder 1938, 1982

Printed and bound in Great Britain by
Cox & Wyman Ltd, Reading

ISBN 0 09 149961 5

The author has drawn upon so many sources for this book that it is impossible to enumerate them, especially as she has accepted no postulate from one source only. She would like here to express her heartfelt thanks and appreciation to all who have helped to make this book possible.

CONTENTS

CONTENTS

ILLUSTRATIONS

PREFACE

These are days in which the spirit of inquiry is perhaps more alive than at any other time in the history of humanity. They are days also in which the orientation of humanity towards spiritual realities and towards the higher values is more pronounced than ever before, in spite of many opinions of the pessimistically inclined to the contrary. The masses are becoming increasingly sensitive to the world of ideas and to the vision of truth. Hitherto it has been the advanced men and women who have so responded, but today it is the many. The spirit in man has always been divinely alive, but today men everywhere are inquiring with one voice: Which is the WAY that we should go? How far have we travelled towards our goal?

This book is an attempt to trace in brief and simple language the progress man has made as he has travelled along the way of truth and thus answer that question. It seeks to penetrate behind the outer world of seeming to the world of spirit, and to find, behind the external forms, that which gives them life.

The subject is necessarily so vast that it is safe to say that it can only be handled in three ways. First by the production of volumes which would embody the erudition of the ages and which would be read, therefore, only by the erudite and selective few. Secondly, by specializing in some one or other of the many aspects of the Ageless Wisdom, and writing on a chosen subject, appealing consequently only to those attracted to that subject and that particular presentation of a part of the truth. Thirdly, by writing simple 'bridging' books which (selecting the highlights in the history of truth and the basic foundational realities) will make the teaching real to the average man in the simplest terms. In this way the man of average intelligence, busy with the affairs of everyday life, can get some understanding of that enlightenment which has ever poured forth over humanity from the heart of God Himself, and thus regain that confidence and that belief in love and immortality which is our divine heritage. This we have somewhat lost through the activity of living, the press of the economic situation, the fear and suspense engendered by the world situation, and the bewilderment aroused in many minds by the warring theologies of the great religions.

As I have read this book, it has seemed to me that the intent of the author is to present to the man in the street (who is now awake and demanding such information) a picture of the two lines of continuity which the history of the past reveals to the attentive student. There is, first of all, the continuity of the Wisdom Teaching, which, down the ages, has come forth from God and thrown the needed light upon the ways of men. It has taken the form outwardly of the world religions (living or dead), but has always presented to those whose eyes were open those esoteric truths and those clear instructions whereby man can find his own soul and his way back to the centre of life. There is, secondly, the continuity of Messengers from the Most High—many little Lightbearers, some great Teachers, and a few perfect Revealers of Divinity, culminating for us in that supreme Son of God Whom Christianity recognizes.

These two interwoven golden threads of light can be seen passing—unbroken and untarnished—down through the history of the race. They are the product of human aspiration and divine response, of human effort and divine transmission. They constitute the way to the goal. They form the Path which all must tread. They indicate the rules which must be followed and they point the way to Those Who have journeyed ahead of us upon the selfsame Path. It is a practical way; it has the endorsement of history and the example of the foremost and the most enlightened who have walked the ways of earth. It is the history of the WAY in contradistinction to the many ways.

There is need for such books as this in the world today, for bridging books which all people can read, which can evoke their interest and lead them to a closer and a more earnest search. This book should find immediately a real field of usefulness and serve and help many. The field of esoteric truth is so large and

its departments so many and so varied that the neophyte is apt
to be confused and bewildered by the extent of the horizon which
opens up before him and the many types of knowledge which
presumably he is expected to master. Mysticism, occultism,
esoteric psychology, astrology, numerology, theosophical doctrines, Kabbalistic lore, Rosicrucian truth, comparative religion,
symbolism and the conflicts between creeds all clamour for his
attention. We need simple synthetic presentations, which
eliminate the non-essentials and give a clear picture in clear outline and clear language. Such a book is this, and, as a forerunner
of many more, I wish it Godspeed and a wide field of service.

ALICE A. BAILEY
1937

AUTHOR'S NOTE 1968

Thirty years have passed since this little book was published. During that time the book and its successors have brought me much rich experience and many friends.

Together we are watching the transition from the old age into the new age, and we are offering our thought and our prayers for the expected event of the 'Second Coming'.

Time rushes by. The old civilization is burning itself up in a crescendo of confusion. But, even before its ashes are formed, the Phoenix can be seen arising, emerging as the new revolting youth of today, in every land—an unprecedented event— universal revolt, seeking, however instinctively, for the Will of God.

If to these new crusaders everywhere could be introduced the Plan of Evolution as it has emerged from all the great Wisdom teachings, they might find an anchor and a purpose by means of which they could lead the world into a new era of both sanity and fulfilment.

It is to this end that this book and its successors are dedicated. The emblem on the cover is a reminder of the instruction from Christ: 'Be ye wise as serpents and harmless as doves!'

VERA STANLEY ALDER

INTRODUCTION

Are human beings potential gods, as they have been told, or are they merely the least of worms?

The world today is a seething mass of contradictions. Life does not become simpler with each new achievement, and the average man, kept busy with the urgent process of existing, has little time for thought.

Yet there are moments when, looking out upon a world which appears drab, cruel, confused, and very ugly in many ways, man wonders . . .

If there *are* great heights for him to attain why does he seem to know so little about them? What has man been doing all these centuries? Why do disease, difficulties and dangers appear to have increased the more civilization 'progresses'?

There comes a time in the lives of many people when they earnestly desire to find an answer to these questions. They would know why they are here, what it is all about, and if they can learn to master circumstances instead of continually being a prey to them. They begin to make an individual effort to find out for themselves if there is really any rhyme or reason, any justice in life, anything to hope for or to work for.

When a man arrives at this stage in his life it marks a very important crisis in his development. It is the moment at which he changes from a puppet into an individual and joins the honoured company of the seekers.

To his surprise he finds that the number of these seekers is increasing rapidly, and that, in fact, they are beginning to make their impact felt upon social consciousness.

He soon sees the significance of this. True socialism becomes possible when people recognize themselves as individual units of power, capability and thought; then there will inevitably follow a correspondingly important and congenial position in life for each one of them. There is an unfailing demand for either the competent worker or for those able to wield constructive influence, and all can fill one of these needs. There is no other way to individual happiness.

The general apathy and ignorance which has existed for so long has reduced living conditions to a chaos in which there has been undernourishment in the midst of plenty, barbaric wars and cruelties taking place under the wing of so-called religion, and a system of education which results neither in mental power, physical fitness, good looks nor happiness.

Now, however, humanity is waking up in a wonderful manner to a recognition of its own failures. Everywhere there is widespread effort and intensive seeking going on in manifold directions. This effort is to be found not only among the leaders and teachers of the people but among the people themselves. The public interest in health, diet, physical culture, spiritualism and hundreds of other cults and movements shows the beginning of a powerful wave of progress which may sweep humanity upwards to the peak of a new Renaissance of a kind the world has never known before.

There are many today already caught in the throes of the birth of this coming Renaissance. They are tormented by the desire to know more of the inner meaning of life and the hidden issues to which they are so swiftly moving. One after another they take up the challenge of Life's Riddle, and join the ever-growing band of seekers.

It is significant that this seeking should press into the realms of 'religious', 'psychic', 'spiritualistic' and 'occult' thought—in other words, the inner unseen world of causes. Man realizes that 'science', which has dealt so successfully with physical phenomena, has not yet succeeded in giving humanity any measure of happiness or safety. So he is at last determined to try to find his happiness by getting in touch with causes instead of effects, by seeking for the laws or truths, if any, which may lie behind the reactions of living things. He begins to sense the difference between knowledge and wisdom.

Knowledge is the result of an accumulation of facts, and its tendency is, through specializing, to isolate subjects one from another.

Wisdom is the deduction from these facts of useful laws, a process which can only take place by comparing the facts in one compartment with those in all the others, thus giving a vision of the whole.

When a man becomes an individual seeker his first effort is to discover what he can of 'facts' connected with the fundamental truths of life. He wants proofs.

There are many people ready to admit him into the world of inner research. He is faced with a long and complicated pilgrimage. Wonderful promises are held out to him; he is assured of becoming a super-man, with health, happiness and power hitherto undreamt-of and hard for him to comprehend. He asks himself if all this can be true. If so, why is humanity still wallowing in such helplessness? In bewilderment he hesitates on the threshold of philosophy, Spiritualism, Christian Science or a dozen other cults and 'isms'!

His inexperienced eyes are unable to detect the true from the false, and he is at the mercy of many people who seek to enlist him for their own pet cult, or who wish to make profit for themselves by trading upon his virgin curiosity and yearning. If he has a tendency to emotionalism or a love of the sensational, he will be an easy prey.

How, then, is he going to escape the many pitfalls and manage to keep upon the true path to an understanding and mastery of life?

These chapters have been written in an effort to provide the seeker with a simple guide-book for his pilgrimage to Truth, a concise and bird's-eye view of the new universe which he is about to explore. It endeavours to help him to place each new discovery into its relevant position so that he, while gathering his store of knowledge, may develop wisdom also, and learn those few essential secrets through which he may attain the poise, power and creativeness which will ultimately develop him into a super-man.

The seekers who acquire and use this knowledge will be the builders of the new and promised Golden Age.

In this book an effort will be made to sort out, summarize and compare the ancient knowledge with modern science. Most of the statements made are capable of world-wide and extensive corroboration by trustworthy authorities, and can be verified by any reader who will care to give the time to it. He can satisfy himself by as many proofs as he has the patience and energy to seek and the intelligence to judge and sift.

The quest after Truth opens up an unimagined and wonderful new world to the seeker, so thrilling and so full of reward and interest that it is not within the power of human speech to portray it. Only the fringe of this absorbing search has been touched in these few pages, but even so this book contains the recipe for turning an ordinary human being into a super-man, one who commands the means of success, happiness or personal fulfilment always within himself, and irrespective of all circumstances.

PART ONE

1

THINGS AS THEY ARE

OUR first concern will be to take a survey of the present position with unprejudiced eyes.

The unprejudiced eye is a much more difficult thing to cultivate than we may imagine. In fact, to most of us it is an impossibility. For generations, indeed for centuries, we have been brought up in certain grooves of thought, certain traditions and habits, until our brains become wedged into a confined rut and are unable to look at things from a new angle.

When, however, after finishing our survey of the present position, we see around us the result of thinking in these grooves, and realize to what a state of unhappiness, chaos and muddle this has brought us, we may, in sheer desperation, make the effort needed to jerk our brains out of their ruts and guard them against ever slipping back again.

Truth can only be understood by one in a state of attention. Therefore Truth is not available to those in a slack condition of mind—they could not take it in. Truth is only to be found 'at the bottom of a well'; it must be struggled for and sought after and come upon through earnest effort, through the stimulation brought about by suffering or striving, whereby the mind is prepared to recognize it.

That is why Truth appears always to be hidden, veiled and guarded.

Let us, then, try to look with new eyes at the struggling mass of inconsistencies which we are in the habit of calling civilization.

Man has striven always for happiness, and he has sought to attain it mostly in one of three ways—comfort, entertainment and religion. But he has sought these things only in their outward form. Comfort for the body has been the first aim, while a comfortable state of mind has been the last thing considered, until the lack of it has reduced the victim to despair. Cleanliness has also been studied outwardly, but seldom in its inward form—we do not understand how to keep our minds wholly free from rubbish and poisoning material. Religion likewise has come to be mostly an external observance, while as for entertainment it is poured in from outside, the mind being required to make no effort to obtain it.

All the same, we are told that Mind over Matter constitutes our real power! Therein is one of the inconsistencies! Let us find some more!

In some countries the State supports a Church which tells us, 'thou shalt not kill', but is not averse to sending us out to war in order to slaughter our possibly blameless fellow-men. For this we are called heroes. Yet if we kill someone for a reason which seems good enough for us we are no longer heroes, and we are hanged!

Many of us are asked to believe in Church teaching and the Bible, both of them containing a mass of contradictions which no one attempts to explain. For example, Christ asked His disciples to carry on the work as He had done, saying: 'He that believeth on me, the works that I do shall he do also; and greater works than these shall he do.'[1] These words referred to healing, prophesying and clairaudience, which, with the 'gift of tongues' (power to be understood by all nationalities), the power to work miracles, to interpret dreams and symbols, and to have wisdom, were the seven gifts of the Holy Ghost. Yet the State, which supports the Church's teachings, may imprison one for pro-phesying, and the clergy, who should be cultivating these gifts, leave them mostly in the hands of those whom they consider ignorant and superstitious.

Calling ourselves civilized, we produce a race which cannot compare with many of the most savage tribes in health and physique. Look around at the members of an average crowd of today and compare them with the Greek ideal, or the early Egyptian or Assyrian bodies. Through unbiased eyes we shall see that we are mostly misshapen travesties of what a human

[1] St. John xiv, 12, *and see* Acts ii, 17.

being should be; we cannot deny the prevalence today of imperfect bodies, unlovely vacant faces, ugly clothes and primitive conversation.

Surely a modern crowd's appearance shrieks of the wrongness of our present mode of living?

We know the hospitals are full; so are the asylums—who dares to tell us how full?

Consider also that we are at present in imminent danger of a world war which would let loose as much beastliness and cruelty as has ever existed in history.

But even without war man is being murdered daily in various ways by the terrible Robot which he has reared under the name of Civilization. This Robot is running amok; it has mastered its creator for the time being and produced a clever system of keeping him in slavery. Much that is really enlightening in knowledge is gradually being eliminated from man's education, which is given to him in odd spoonfuls having no apparent relation to each other. Through no fault of his own he is under an economic system which causes him to spend all his days in the terror and anxiety of being without means of support. If he works at all he must drudge the whole week through, while many of his comrades are refused employment, and he is obliged to pay for their support; there is 'over-production' and yet a difficulty in obtaining cheap food, even in some countries the danger of starvation; honesty and purity are preached to him from one side, while pornography and sensationalism are showered upon him from the other.

Every effort is made to soak him through and through with an interest in sex—by means of cinemas, theatres, books, newspapers and through the type of food most cheaply obtained. He is never told the plain truth—that a preoccupation with sex is one of the greatest deterrents to brain development.

He is surrounded with mind-destroying noise, rush and anxiety, until even the doctors are beginning to say that modern life will soon exterminate itself!

As if this were not enough, he is furthermore at the mercy of the war-lords, who can send him out to murder and mangle his fellow-men even if he has the kindest character; and, escaping this last horror, he is daily slaughtered in his own streets by his brother road-hogs, while they, in turn, pay millions into the hospitals to put him together again!

Life altogether seems to have been expressly planned to prevent him from creative thought; he has been, until quite recently, offered no problems to solve; his entertainment has been put before him in the form of predigested sensationalism— mental baby-food.

Weary and half drugged by this intensive treatment, man has largely ceased to recognize the heritage of his wonderful mind. He no longer knows why he should think—or what there is to think about.

Here then is a pessimistic picture of life as it is today!

Ought we to be satisfied with this state of affairs? Is this indeed the whole picture, or is there a brighter side to it?

Let us not forget the claim that man is a marvellous creature, in spite of much that appears to the contrary. This claim seems not to be entirely without foundation. On every hand we find clues to strange and tremendous forces hidden within us, forces that when properly understood and developed could certainly lead us to unimaginable power and achievement. We glimpse these powers in such people as the imaginative genius, the child prodigy, the thought-reader, the healer and the clairvoyant. We hear of them on every side and their existence is too well known to be disputed.

There are many great men alive today whose achievements stand out in sharp contrast to the average. Is it that they are super-men, or that the rest of us are lagging far behind the point of development we should have reached? If we were to lay any of them upon the dissecting-table we should certainly find nothing about them that differs in any degree from the average person.

Where, then, is the key to the wonderful power and omnipotence that apparently may be every man's birthright? There is nothing to prove that we could not all attain complete mastery over our lives and fortunes, and reach ideal happiness, were we given this key, and had the will and the determination to use it. Had we this secret, instead of being, as we are, slaves to life, to our possessions, our environment, ill-health, 'bad luck' and the rest, we could be master and controller of all our circumstances, and welcome with content and understanding everything that life brings to us.

We are told that the secret lies in the use and understanding of a certain knowledge through which is given an insight into the inner laws and forces of life, and the manner in which to use them. This knowledge has always existed, but it remains hidden for ever from all but the earnest seeker.

For the last few hundred years humanity has been passing through its Slough of Despond—Ignorance.

The hour has already struck which marks the beginning of humanity's emergency from that blackness. Men have suffered so much and for so long, through ignorance, that at last the inevitable reaction has set in. We can feel this change beginning to play in subtle ways through all phases of life.

We have reached the time when we demand to *know*, and to know for ourselves and through ourselves, and to wield that knowledge irrespective of authority. We refuse any longer to dance like puppets to the drugging jazz tunes of incompetent authority. And soon authority will have to pull itself together and follow the lead of the seekers.

For there is widespread seeking going on everywhere now for the happiness, freedom and power which we instinctively feel will be ours when we have gained the requisite knowledge.

And the knowledge is to be found—hidden, waiting, wonderful!

Our first clue to this knowledge lies in the study of what is known as the Secret Wisdom. This teaching was always in the charge (in the early days) of those who were well equipped both to govern and teach. But in time they neglected their deep knowledge in favour of the easier way—power through money, superstition and material pomp. This resulted in laziness and effete degeneration. Their only hope of retaining hold on the people was to plunge them into ignorance also. Therefore a systematic persecution of certain knowledge began, by edicts, inquisitions and massacres. Finally their end was so thoroughly attained that from the highest to the lowest the wisdom had apparently faded out.

Fortunately, however, there are now, and always have been, those who would give their whole lives to the guarding and hiding of a treasure so precious. Such people were the al-chemists, hermits, early freemasons and many more. So the knowledge was not really lost, but only concealed and safely guarded from desecration.

Humanity is fast approaching the day when, through patient struggling, it will have earned the right to this wisdom; in fact, some years ago it was given out in part for those earnest seekers in the vanguard of progress to discover. Let us make all speed to gain for ourselves this rich heritage.

Whether we approach the subject from a purely scientific viewpoint, from a common-sense one, or from a religious one, we will find that science, logic or the root-form of any of the principal religions will lead us finally to identical truths. We will realize that if we are able to accept these truths we will obtain a very satisfactory understanding of the 'workings' of Nature', and of certain rules which will enable us to control ourselves and our circumstances in a manner hitherto impossible.

We cannot gain such valuable knowledge without making worthy effort, but if we persevere there is no limit to the benefit we shall obtain.

The earliest results achieved will be, firstly, a considerable improvement and control of health and looks, a growing capacity for happiness, an inability to worry or fear; a gaining of popu-larity, and freedom from boredom.

In time, when greater strides are made, there will be immunity from disease, conquering of fatigue, and prolonging of youth. There will be a growing capacity for helping others, a mastery of sorrow and pain, and the development of healing power. A growing inner force will be felt, both for creating ideas and the carrying of them out.

Neither does the tale end here. Very advanced students, such as are the Yogis, become unaffected by heat or cold, wounds and poisons. They are able to perform feats usually considered as miracles, and they appear to have access to regions of wisdom and felicity undreamt of by us. People of this type move about among us unsuspected. They do not advertise themselves; they are under a Law which forbids them to help unless help is asked, or to give out knowledge unless it is sought and will be properly understood. They are ready and waiting for the time when a growing number of people sense their secrets and beg their help.

When the general public have sufficiently advanced they will insist on being governed by persons of such attainments, and then indeed will begin the coming Golden Age.

Meanwhile those who are anxious to forge ahead and prepare for the future will find in this book a broad survey of many sides of the subject, together with the first simple rules for the beginning of attainment.

They are asked only to keep an open mind as they read, for only an open mind is big enough to contain the secrets of the universe.

2

WHAT MODERN SCIENCE SAYS

BEFORE we begin studying the ancient wisdom we will find it very helpful to prepare our minds by taking a survey of the ground covered by modern science today. It will be fascinating to see how identical facts can be known under different names and reached by different methods.

Both the ancient sages and modern scientists are agreed that everything in life is formed of vibrations. So that, as we shall be obliged often to use this word, we can begin by defining it.

We are told that vibration is the result of force or energy, concentrated in some mysterious way and caused to vibrate, shake or oscillate at different speeds. The composition of an atom, according to some scientists, is, first of all, a tiny vacuum, round which this force or energy revolves as a vortex, just as the circle of the sun's aura or zodiac revolves round it. The zodiac contains the planets revolving within it, and the minute 'zodiac' of the atom contains also its planets, or electrons as they are called.

The difference between one object and another is ultimately a question of rate of vibration. It is the number and arrangement of the electrons within an atom, and the varied cohesions of atoms into molecules, which go to make up these vibratory differences.

The disturbance in the atmosphere caused by a vibration sends out a ripple or air-wave in all directions. As an illustrative simile of this we can throw a stone into a pool of water. At first we see the hole which the stone makes, corresponding to the vacuum in the centre of the atom. Then we see the disturbance in the water created by the hole, a circle of energy which sets up waves or ripples which spread out to an unlimited distance.

Drop other stones in nearby, and their circle of waves will flow over and through the others, none, however, being destroyed although they affect one another slightly. The distance between one ripple and the next is called the 'wave-length'.

We have in this a rough picture of what happens in the atmosphere, and of the waves set up by light, sound, or any kind of object—anything, in other words, that vibrates.

Low rates of vibration form the more static or visible objects; we might say that they send out only slow ripples; higher rates of motion, between the rapidly flying particles, form less tangible things, such as gas. These particles intermingle rapidly with the air, but often they do not move sufficiently quickly to penetrate through solids.

I would like to say here that the statements in this chapter are not intended to be scientific accuracies, but roughly suggestive for the purposes of our argument. As the 'facts' of science are continually having to be modified or changed we need not take them too seriously. The last word has never been said!

Vibrations of a relatively low frequency are known to us as sounds. Higher ranges are known as heat.

Sound and heat are fine enough to pass through certain solids. We know all about the ripples or waves caused by sound. So also we know about the electrical impulses, through the wireless, and we call them wave-lengths, and know all their measurements. Some of the wireless wave-lengths are as much as three miles long.

We might picture the scale of vibrations as a vast keyboard, on which there are many octaves and different types of vibration and motion. One range of motion expresses itself as solid, liquid and gaseous forms. Other ranges are perceived as sound, heat and those intangible things about which we know little.[1]

Above the octaves of sound would come those of light and colour vibrations. The colours range from red—the lowest (which vibrates at 451 million million times per second, and has a wave-length of one 36,918th of an inch)—up to violet. We see this order of colours in the rainbow and in the spectrum.

[1] *Rosicrucian Cosmo-Conception*, see table, p. 255.

Above the violet, colour can no longer be seen by the eye, and we find the ultra-violet rays and the X-ray. Now at last we have reached vibrations fine and rapid enough to penetrate through most solids. Higher up on the scale we come to the magnetic vibrations and their wave-lengths, such as those that issue from the mind of the hypnotist. These can go through denser solids than the X-ray can, which accounts for the hypnotist being able to produce the effect of a deep trance upon a person seated in an adjoining room.

Apparently the vibrations of the mind can travel instantaneously many hundreds of miles, as in thought telepathy, passing through all solids which intervene. They have an intimate connection with electricity which, as we know, can travel round the world in a flash.

Each thought is a vibration having a set wave-length! When, however, we consider the vastness of the scale of vibrations with which we have to deal it will be seen that there are enough and to spare for everything.

Now, having placed sound, light and heat in their respective order as we know it, we must ask what they are and how we know they exist.

Had we and the animals no ears, what would sound be?

What we know as sound is that tiny section of octaves on the scale of vibration which can be transmitted to the brain by the receivers in the ear. The human ear is successful up to a certain point, beyond which it can receive no more; but many animals hear vibrations which to us are no longer sounds at all.

Higher up on our keyboard than sound comes heat. Our skin contains the little receivers to transmit these vibrations, to which the ear is no longer sensible.

Farther up the scale still we come to light and colour. We only have one tiny marvellous organ to register this set of vibrations to the brain—the optic nerve. The eye is made to react up the scale of colour to the violet vibration. After that, as already stated, the oscillation is so minute and rapid that it can interpenetrate solids, so these ultraviolet vibrations pass right through the eye lens.

The question now arises—have we any organs which can deal with those higher vibrations, or the very subtle substance of which they are composed, and in what form are these contacted?

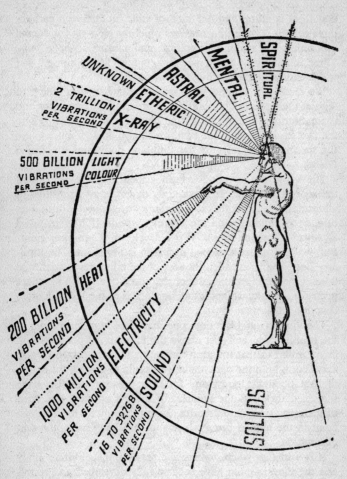

MAN'S RESPONSE TO VIBRATIONS

These last vibrations are so fine that they use the ether as their vehicle instead of the heavier air particles. The ether is that indefinable substance in which this earth and all the atoms of the air are supported. Scientists are on the verge of discovering that there is more than one kind of ether, in fact even perhaps three or four. The finest vibrations which we have yet considered are within the realm of electrical and magnetic phenomena. These are the forces which man also contains within himself, and which can be utilized through the mind.

We must now inquire what organs man has with which to register these particular vibrations, embracing the radiations and emanations which come under the general term 'psychic'. There are two small glands in the head which give doctors much cause for speculation. I refer to the Pituitary Body and the Pineal Gland.

The former is a tiny, double bean-shaped body situated behind the root of the nose. It is posed so that it is very sensitive to vibrations. We know that it is in some way connected with nurture, body-building, and the nervous system. If it is removed all organic function ceases. If overdeveloped it produces giantism, while if underdeveloped dwarfism is the result. The Pituitary Body has been called the seat of the mind. Its frontal lobe is concerned with emotional thought, of the type which produces poetry and music, while the anterior lobe is connected with more concrete intellectual concepts.

The Pineal Gland is a tiny cone-shaped body in the middle of the head, behind and just above the Pituitary. It contains pigment similar to that found in the eyes, and is connected by two nerve cords with the optic thalmi; it is said to control the action of light upon the body, and for these reasons scientists have suggested that it is the remnant of a third physical eye. Men of learning, such as Descartes, have pronounced it to be the point in the human being where soul and body meet, the seat of intuition.

It is said that when, for specific reasons, the Pituitary Body and the Pineal Gland have become fully developed and stimulated, their vibrations fuse and stir into life the mysterious 'Third

Eye' of man, the eye of the soul. Apparently this activity provides the mind with a perfect instrument with which to work, a transmitter by means of which vibrations of very differing types can be translated, interpreted and rearranged. This gives him personal access to much knowledge, of which we will speak later.

Man can also become sensitive to the finer chemical and magnetic emanations in the ether, and can 'see' the numberless thought-forms, entities and creatures, the endless complexities and types of life which make up a vast world of teeming energies which the limited capacity of ordinary physical sight is unable to register.

In a few people there is a slight involuntary functioning of these latter activities, and we call them either clairvoyant or crazy, according to our understanding. They can literally see the radiations and 'photographs' in the ether which are given off by almost any kind of body. We will study these in a later chapter. But, just as the muscles and brain need developing in an average person, so these organs of 'second sight' need their own particular training. Many, however, are born with a 'knack' for their use, in the way of any other type of prodigy.

When a psychometrist holds an article to his forehead against the awakened 'Third Eye' it tunes in to and commingles with the vibrations emanating from the article, and as these vibrations represent a certain picture, just as do our thoughts, he is able to describe the associations attached to it. The emanations from an object are often so fine and numerous that they continue to be given off for thousands of years, just as with radium.

The Egyptians knew all about the 'Third Eye', and indicated it on the statues of their gods by a knob on the forehead. They trained the people in the use of this psychic centre in the temple of Ma-at. The god Ma-at was vulture-headed, because the vulture has a sight so keen as to be almost clairvoyant. When people responded to this training they became 'seers', or psychic, as we should say now. They could see with the trained 'Third Eye' right through a body, as the X-ray does, and diagnose disease. All over the East we find statues of historic men or women of wisdom with a knob or other mark upon the forehead indicating this type of achievement.

Of course there are some people who have this power today, but we do not understand its use nor how to train them properly, consequently their development has been left to chance.

We have now reached the most subtle portion on the scale of vibrations which we are discussing. The question arises as to whether we have quite exhausted its possibilities, or whether there are still finer ones than those that exist in the ether, and, if so, have we any means of contacting them?

The sphere of thought next occurs to us. We are told that 'thoughts are things'! We know that each thought has its definite vibration, because this has been proved. An instrument has been invented by Dr. Baraduc of Bordeaux which records thought vibrations. When an intelligent person approaches this instrument it registers a high-speed and strong vibration. When a low type or imbecile approaches it the vibration is correspondingly feeble and slow.

It has also been proved by experiment that by an act of will the mind can cause objects such as metal levers to move (see experiments by Sir William Crookes in *Edinburgh Lectures on Mental Science*). We have also heard of numberless cases of fakirs and people of that kind having been able to prevent themselves from burning by fire, from suffocating when buried alive, from bleeding from wounds, and from other normal reactions. They can do this by being able to bring into action the power that the finer vibrations of the mind have over the lower ones of chemical matter. The same thing is done in chemistry through the use of electrical heat to split up, reorganize or control chemical compounds.

Sometimes people use these powers without knowing exactly what they are doing, nor what the result will be, as in the cases of some forms of mental healing, based on 'blind faith'. Such cases are a wonderful proof of existing possibilities, but at best they are uncertain (sometimes only 'flukes'), and often much harm is done through lack of a fuller understanding.

In curing some diseases, either by self-treatment or by a mental healer, the fine vibrations of the mind act on the lower vibrations of the disease tissue. This can be performed at the same rate at which that particular mind is able to visualize and concentrate—it may take hours, days or weeks, according to the condition of patient and healer.

However, we know that there have occurred many cases of 'instantaneous' healing, diseased and broken tissues being rendered whole in a flash of time. We have heard of such things throughout history, and they are said to happen at the present day in places such as Lourdes. In these cases we have at last touched upon the finest and subtlest 'vibrations' of all, those of the 'spirit' or the highest creative force. Such vibrations, being unhampered by the processes of the brain, and operating at a terrific speed, can go through the whole process of cure so quickly that we cannot possibly follow its course, and the result seems to us to be instantaneous.

With a great spiritual healer such as Christ was, works of this kind are possible, especially if the sufferer can tune in, through 'faith' or through the medium of his own 'spiritual' vibrations, to the healer's actions. Christ encouraged us to strive for these powers of healing, which are not really 'supernatural', but the result of an intensive development and an understanding of the laws of the universe.

The mind has power over everything that it can understand and visualize. Therefore the first step of all is to study these arguments and theories, and those facts which are supported by adequate testimony, with a perfectly open and logical mind.

If and when we become convinced of any argument or concept, we must tabulate it carefully, and pass on to a study of the next. In this way we will begin gradually to discover what we really *can* know and believe.

For instance, we may feel that it is impossible for us to prove for ourselves the truth of Christ's miracles, or of any others in the past. But actually such things are happening every day, in every guise and form, and a little inquiry will soon put us in touch with them. Our own common sense will then enable us to separate the true from the false.

The object of this chapter is to show that, although we may

approach this subject from the angle of pure chemical and mechanical science, we shall still be able to work through to the final result that there is a certain force controlled by our minds which can act more powerfully over solid matter than anything else; and that there is a still stronger force, apparently outside of mind, which can act instantaneously and 'miraculously'.

It is not enough to go on any longer weakly tabulating these things as 'hypnotism', 'thought-reading', or 'imagination'. They must be better understood for what they really are. We must have an explanation for the changes in tissue and matter which occur. The old alchemists claimed that it was possible to direct a mental force to change the composition of atoms by altering their vibrations, and that thereby it would be possible to make gold. They believed it was so, but already materialism had stepped in, and they often endeavoured to accomplish it by chemical means alone.

The only real power to do such things lies within ourselves, but we must first learn to use our own highest vibrations.

These powers can only work if they are undisturbed by the inharmonious heavy vibrations which enter into our composition if we live out of harmony with the laws of Nature.

The athlete knows that alcohol, smoking, unbalanced diet, worry and lack of sleep upset his health and undermine his stamina, so that even the low vibrations of physical strength and steadiness cannot gain control.

The mental worker knows that he has to steady down all his bodily disturbances and vibrations before he can concentrate at all. He needs not only to be able to ignore the vibrations all around him, which he can only do if they are steady and balanced (a hum of traffic disturbs many much less than odd drops of falling water), but also he must have steadiness and balance of every activity of his own body—so that he can ignore it.

If, however, he is seeking neither athletic nor mental expression, but 'inspiration', he can only obtain that by steadying down the brain itself, so that, balancing its vibrations to the same state of poise as those of his body, he can ignore the brain and reach for the subtler forces of the mind. The greatest inspiration will flash suddenly into the brain at a moment when it is quiet and receptive.

Therefore, although the highest vibrations are the most powerful, we cannot get in touch with them within ourselves when our bodies and brains are a mass of struggling, fighting inharmonious vibrations, as is usually the case. Though the highest forces are there within us, we give ourselves little chance of linking up with them, and consequently are unable to utilize them.

The yogis and fakirs spend hours in 'meditation', or the effort to quieten down every activity in the body and brain, so that the aforementioned portions of the latter, the Pineal Gland and the Pituitary Body, can 'tune in' to those highest powers. When this is accomplished these men can, while in that state, cure their own and others' bodily or mental ills, obtain inspiration or wisdom, and attain a high state of physical fitness and strength without our methods of 'exercise'.

The first thing for us to do, therefore, is to eliminate all inharmonious vibrations from our bodies and brains. We must throw them out one by one as we discover them. Every unnecessary act, thought, emotion and fear must go! We must build into the fabric of our lives only those things which will balance, strengthen, and beautify them. We will find that there is a tremendous amount of accumulated rubbish to cast away! Those things which remain will give us all the greater joy and interest through being intensified.

The simple methods for doing this will be explained later.

Before closing this chapter let us give a thought to the modern scientists. Having followed a long trail in their efforts to discover the difference between matter and the life which pours through it, they have finally arrived at the perplexing result that there is no difference at all! They now know that solid matter in its final analysis is merely energy in a certain state of motion. They also know that our thoughts are also energy in a certain state of motion!

In other words, the world appears to be made up of the energy of the Being or Mind behind it, whose idea it was!

The scientists do not put it this way—yet!

From a scientific point of view they have come up against a blank wall, and their present attitude is probably that of a big question-mark.

3

THE SECRET KNOWLEDGE

HAVING studied our world according both to the modern matter-of-fact scientist and the less orthodox modern ideas, let us now turn and plunge into the past, and see what our ancestors knew, and how their knowledge helped them.

They prophesied the long dark Age of Ignorance from which we are at present emerging. That ignorance has engendered in us the habit of scoffing at everything which is not 'ordinary', 'normal' or able to be weighed and measured by scientists.

The scientists themselves have reached a point where they are no longer dealing with purely physical or chemical things—they have pushed upwards through the great scale of vibrations until their heads are in the clouds of conjecture. Perhaps they dare not speak of the possibilities they conceive.

Let us leave them hesitating in that exciting position, and start a tour of exploration on our own.

In a universe full of trillions of stars, of constellations and solar systems, there is one minute little revolving speck of matter which we call our earth. This speck of matter is covered with millions of microscopical creatures called human beings. The strange thing is that these microscopical creatures consider themselves important. Each minute one of them is able to feel that he is more important than the whole universe upon which he is but a speck.

Are these creatures really important, and if so, why?

Looking at them dispassionately, we can see that there is at least one remarkable thing about them. Almost any one of them, by training his microscopical brain, is able to visualize the past, present and future, not only of his own little person, country or planet, but of the whole universe. Within his tiny personality there is locked a power which will give him unlimited understanding of things quite beyond his physical reach, a dynamic capacity to wield the forces of Nature with a mind of which he knows not the limits.

Man is an animal, but he is an animal embodying a god. The ancients were much more alive to his potentialities than we are now. As we explore, it will take us some time to decide whether man knew more thousands of years ago than he does today, and whether he was a finer being.

This planet is infinitely older than most of us imagine, and so is the history of mankind. Archaeologists are continually having to push back their dates further into the past. Much learnt in history books by the last generation is obsolete, and must now be unlearnt! Civilizations had been rising, falling and disappearing aeons before the men who owned the paleolithic skulls were born.

All these things are revealed to us in the Ancient or Secret Wisdom, which is a collection of teachings handed down from the very earliest times, explaining man, his origin, his composition and destiny, and also the purpose of the Universe. The Wisdom has come to us in unchanged form, concealed and taught throughout the world under the garb of many of the ancient religions. We will trace this in a later chapter, but begin now by a study of the Wisdom itself as it is still to be found in the East.

This teaching professes to expound to us the few great fundamental laws upon which are founded the life and progress of man and the universe.

Let us endeavour to shake off the habits of thought imposed upon us by the generations of a Dark Age, and consider with an open mind the heritage bequeathed to us by our earlier ancestors.

The Great Laws can best be named for us in English as follows:

(1) REPETITION: THE MICROCOSM AND THE MACROCOSM.
(2) EVOLUTION.

(3) CAUSE AND EFFECT, OR 'KARMA' AND REBIRTH.

(4) THE PLAN OF CREATION, OR THE SEVEN PLANES.

The principle of the first of these Laws is: 'As in the Microcosm (man) so in the Macrocosm (the universe).' It asserts that the same system of form, time and motion runs through the whole universe, so that if we properly study an atom or a cell we will obtain the key to the workings of a man, a planet, or a constellation. In that way, through a knowledge of periodicity—or the regular periods of time which occur on a small scale in nature—the ancient mathematicians were able to calculate the stars, their movements, and thereby the evolutionary stages in history on a large scale, and to prophesy conditions and influences thousands of years ahead.

It is disconcerting to find that the conceptions of the very ancient sages tax the modern man's mind to the utmost. Even to understand their meaning and visualize their ideas takes effort and practice—much less could modern man originate such profound theories himself. And the ancients accomplished these things without, so far as we know, any of our modern mechanical aids.

This great Law of Repetition declares that there is an ordered arrangement within the universe, with certain periods of time and patterns of form repeated up the scale and governing the tiniest to the greatest. It asserts that the little things are a mirror of the larger ones, and everything is not only a replica but intimately connected with everything else. For instance, if you want to study a solar system you can study an atom. And if you want to study animal, plant, mineral or even solar life you will find it all represented in the body of man himself.

'Man, Know Thyself' was the ancient command written above the temple door. If we persevere with this fascinating study we will find that in the form of every human being the universe is presented to us; we can inspect the solar systems of his atoms, the mineral world in its most active and creative form in his interior laboratory, and the physical development of animal life from its lowest to its highest form in his embryo. In his nature we will find a mixture of the passions and peculiarities of all living creatures. We can also trace an intimate relationship with all the planets through the interplay going on in his body with the cosmic and planetary rays, and a connection with the world of magnetism and electricity as well. Finally we will discover that man has in his puny frame the capacity to connect his mind with the highest unseen cosmic intelligence—the mind of 'Nature'.

This first great Law, then, that of the Macrocosm and the Microcosm, gives us at once a much more comprehensive outlook on life, and therefore the capacity of bringing vision and breadth into our creative work.

The second great Law is that of EVOLUTION:

Everything in life is evolving upwards and onwards to a higher and more perfect state, having had its beginning in an uncreative, unconscious and elementary form, and growing and progressing through striving, sacrifice and struggle to a condition of creative selfconscious potent strength.

Beginning at the lowest end of the scale with the minerals, we know that they have an elementary consciousness or mentality; that they strive, struggle and become tired, and that they are 'sacrificed' to or absorbed by the kingdom above them, the vegetable kingdom which lives upon them.

The vegetable kingdom has a higher consciousness or vibration than the mineral kingdom, and a greater power for struggling and adapting itself; in its turn it is sacrificed to the animal kingdom who feed upon it. The animals may seem to the plants to be some kind of deities, with wonderful and to them 'miraculous' powers of movement.

The sum of vegetable and mineral experience is absorbed by the animals, who depend on this for their life and evolution. In return, it is said that the animals provide, by their breathing, the carbondioxide upon which plants exist during the day. Some of the animals are becoming extremely advanced in consciousness, and are full of what can be described as (for them) spiritual aspiration. Mankind are their deities, and they strain and strive to attain, in such things as speech and work, to the miraculous activities of their gods. The adoring eyes of a dog and his efforts to talk, and the keenness and pride of an elephant at work, are instances in point.

Animals in their turn offer up their sacrifice of adoration, emulation and service to man. Whereas the vegetable kingdom should adequately sustain the body of man, the animal kingdom should feed his emotional needs *only*, through his function of guardianship ('dominion') over them. This relationship of loving, learning and teaching is the true one, instead of the prevailing extraordinary exploitation, slaughter and cruelty enacted towards animals, which forms the basis of similar attitudes towards all the other kingdoms, producing the predatory world which we have today.

We continue up the scale and find that in the kingdom of man the same process is going on. The more advanced type of human being is sacrificing his lower nature, and striving to reach and copy a higher kingdom of beings than his own. He calls these beings angels, gods or deities, and has as much difficulty in understanding their wonderful capabilities as the animals have in understanding his own. But just as the animals depend upon man for the final development of their intelligence, so man depends upon the subtler and more inspiring minds of the 'angels' for his own awakening.

We are told, also, that, just as man depends for his sustenance and progress upon the lower kingdoms of nature, so the 'angel' world depends upon the offering and sacrificing of man's 'soul-force' for its own nourishing and development. Mankind and the angels can only reach greater heights of realization through the interplay of mutual service.

In accordance with the first great Laws of Repetition we realize that the process must continue, and therefore we are bound to infer that the angels are also sacrificing to, and striving to reach, a higher kingdom of Beings than themselves.

The Ancient Wisdom has mapped out for us the pattern of these angel communities and Hierarchies. An amazing vista of worlds ahead of us is thereby opened up for our consideration.

The third great Law is that of KARMA AND REBIRTH. This states that nothing in life is wasted, and all things share alike the chance of gaining ultimate perfection and of going through the full course of experience and development. We see that in the physical world as soon as a plant or other living creature has had its particular span of life it dies or withers. The cells which formed it disintegrate, but their chemical constituents come together at a later period to form a future plant or animal, closely resembling the former one, but plus, *always*, a stage of further adaptability, and change, showing that the consciousness and memory of the former plant has been reborn too.

When we come to a highly specialized consciousness like that of a human being we are told that it is being continually reborn upon the earth, and that it struggles and strives upwards perfecting and developing itself through numberless hard lessons and inevitable mistakes, until finally it reaches the stage of creative and conscious power which we call 'superhuman'.

The method by which experience and progress is assured is expressed in the ancient law of KARMA. This word has not even an equivalent in the English language. Its meaning is 'cause-and-effect', or 'action-and-reaction'. We are told that all of life is built upon the law of opposites, as in the negative and positive poles of electricity, day and night, heat and cold, summer and winter, good and evil. The constant friction between these opposites causes development, change, adjustment—in other words originality, or the free-will which functions throughout all creation, and through which creation itself learns eventually to become creative.

All this happens so slowly (to us) that at times we do not realize that there is progress, because we become confused by the backward crouch of the wave of progress before a further push forward. Probably we are living at the time of a backward crouch now, and perhaps that is why so much that is bad in humanity seems to be driven to the surface, so that to some the world appears at present to be deteriorating.

The Laws of Rebirth and Karma work hand in glove, so to speak. We are told that mankind came into being because Spirit, or the life-force behind everything, wished to develop more creative power. This development could only be accomplished by Spirit being so imprisoned and confined in matter (flesh) that It forgets Its oneness with Wisdom, and has to find everything out afresh through fighting and experience. So we are told that Virgin Spirit divided itself up into fractions and, by ensouling the egos of man and all other forms of life, sank itself into the heavy imprisoning matter of this world, and is slowly and patiently fighting its way back to Truth and Light and Power. The human egos evolve steadily, each undergoing constant rebirth, until it gradually attains to a knowledge of the laws of the universe through Karma—or the effect of its own acts and thoughts, achieving power and strength through the mastery of one law after another until at last it reaches omnipotence both physical and spiritual. We might say that the friction between the opposite poles of spirit and flesh causes, as in electricity, light or energy, which is creative force-power! The planets, the earth, the races of mankind, the animal, vegetable and mineral kingdoms also reincarnate, all being under the same law. (We must mention here that it is not possible, according to the Secret Teaching, for man to be reborn as an animal, because however low he might sink in his own kingdom he could not retrogress into a slower vibration. This theory, called Transmigration of Souls, is held by certain peoples who have allowed their former knowledge to become distorted.)

Many persons here in the West find it rather difficult to accept this theory of reincarnation, because it has been stamped out for thousands of years. It therefore requires a great deal of unaccustomed mental exercise to obtain a real picture of it to hold in the mind. It is accepted quite naturally by most of the Eastern peoples, and has been for untold centuries, so that whether we believe in it or not we should go into the theory as fairly and impartially as if we were studying their ideas on art or agriculture.

As a rule human beings are unable to remember anything about any past lives they may have had. Of course there are exceptions, and many people have collected a great deal of evidence of such memories, which evidence is extremely interesting. In fact, I think we would find it impossible to deny that *some* people, at least, have lived before. When we consider that we are unable to remember a great deal of our present life, especially things which have affected our characters deeply, until they are laid bare by a psycho-analyst, it is not surprising if we do not remember past lives. But we are told that the experience gained in such lives is retained by us in those qualities which we describe as 'having a conscience', an 'instinct' or a 'knack'.

According to this, then, a child prodigy is the result of continuous effort in past lives along some particular line. It might reasonably follow that imbecility is the result of a continuous refusal to use the brain and make effort; that to be a dwarf or cripple is the Karma of one who in previous lives neglected his body; and that an epileptic is probably discharging the debt of continuous immorality in a past life. In the light of this reasoning we could feel that there is no injustice or inequality in life, because the egos are choosing their own ways of learning life's lessons, which can only be learnt through experience and suffering. Believing this, then, we could blame our parents for nothing since we are the masters of our own fate, and reap exactly as we have sown in the past—the effect of the cause—Karma!

We are told that certain groups of people incarnate together at intervals. In this way old injuries and insults must be recompensed, old enmities finally adjusted, and old loves allowed to continue and to grow and beautify. Nothing is lost, nothing is wasted, everyone finally reaches the same goal of perfection, although they are all in such different stages and classes now. No man becomes perfect or attains his goal so long as there is a single feeling of enmity between him and another, or until a score has been settled and wiped out by service and friendship. This is what Christ meant when He gave us that difficult injunction to 'turn the other cheek' and to 'offer thy cloak also to him who shall take thy coat'. If we 'love our neighbour as ourselves' we cannot mind to whom the coat belongs! These conceptions are very difficult for a selfish world to grasp as yet, and few of us have the pluck to try them out.

We limit ourselves by being possessive. The greatest things we can have—wisdom, health and power—are all-pervading, and cannot be divided. They can only develop and be shared. Possessiveness, on the other hand, causes wars, cruelties, jealousies and sufferings. It can never do any good, and usually despoils the most beautiful thing in life—Love.

Therefore, if we can once believe in Reincarnation we would realize that Fear is wasted effort, because though we have suffered death and pain often before we are here again! Fear is something of our making, and it paralyses us and renders us stupid.

Also we can see that it is better not to think evil, unkind or worried thoughts, because by doing so we are *causing effects* which we will have a lot of work in putting right again—Karma! Thoughts are things, and when we unloose an ugly or harmful thing into the world we shall be obliged to remove it. Thoughts persist in the ethereal regions, and are connected with the one who made them until they are disintegrated through his effort.

The fourth great Law is that of the PLAN OF CREATION which teaches us about the Seven Planes. We learn that the whole of the solar system is built upon an orderly numerical system, and a set of seven definitely graded types of matter, substance, or, as the mystics and occultists call them, planes. These planes meet one another in a delicately graded sequence of interpenetrating vibrations with which the modern scientist is experimenting today and which we discussed in Chapter 2. The scope of his discoveries lies roughly between the phenomenon of sound (with its lowest vibration at about sixteen to the second) to that of X-ray (whose highest vibrations are estimated at 2,305,843,009,213,693,952 per second). These vibrations constitute a portion of what is known as the chemical or physical world or plane. The ancients were able to understand and tabulate seven times as much as this, because they postulated seven worlds of different kinds of life, interpenetrating and influencing one another, through which were functioning the various life-forces, currents, rays, thoughts, emotions, and archetypes of form which combine to produce life as it is, with all its different complexities. They had all this thoroughly worked out, and understood just how these different forces were concentrated into man's body through the channels of his various glands. The doctors of today are still struggling with the 'unknown' functions of some of these glands because they have not had the inspiration to refer to the ancient knowledge and unravel the symbolism in which it was presented.

This symbolism was arranged and used both to awe the public and keep them from a knowledge which might be dangerous when in the hands of the ignorant and unprincipled, in much the same way as Latin is employed today by doctors. In times of high national morale more and more of the secrets were given out and understood by the public. But in periods of decadence and materialism the priests and rulers themselves deteriorated, and the knowledge was hidden away and guarded by the few remaining initiates or sages.

We are emerging from a long period of such materialism at present, and that is why doctor, priest and public are confronted with the task of learning a great deal all over again, and revising the knowledge of their ancestors before they can carry things a step further.

This revision was begun at the end of last century by such people as Madame Blavatsky through the Theosophists, by the Christian Scientists, by Mesmer, and a host of others, who aroused the public desire to penetrate once more into the fundamental meaning of Life and its ultimate purpose. Since then modern methods have been used to unearth the Ancient Wisdom and once more reinstate it.

Some people say, 'What do we want with the past? Let us go forward and be practical!' But as we have not yet been able to improve in some respects upon the conceptions of art, architecture, mathematics, ethics, and science of some of those very ancient civilizations to any degree, it will surely be worth our while to study the foundations upon which their mentalities were built.

The four Great Laws which we have enumerated in this chapter were a part of those foundations.

We hear people say, 'Oh, the East is degenerate and effeminate, and social conditions there are terrible—therefore, of what use has that Ancient Wisdom been?' People like this should think further, realizing that the higher one mounts the lower one can fall. Degeneracy is the result of laziness, slackness and subsequent distortion of teaching, and has nothing whatever to do with the pure teaching of a religion in its original form, which is nearly always fine. We have only to consider the original teaching of Christ, observing how we have degenerated that, with our long history of bloodshed, greed and oppression, to feel that we cannot point any finger of criticism at the East. Also, the East is now the prey of old age, and feminine in character, as compared with the vigorous, youthful, masculine Western civilization.

The four Great Laws are hidden in the Christian religion, and can be revealed with a little study, in spite of the mistranslation and censorship to which it has been subjected.

It is very necessary to see life as a Whole, and realize that we can obtain a high state of mental balance and vision only when we attempt to link together the past, present and future, and all the sciences, into one comprehensive and comprehensible picture.

4

HOW WE ARE MADE

THE secret knowledge explains to us in quite a scientific way how we are made.

We have seen that modern scientists have worked out the whole of physical or chemical life to a scale of atoms vibrating at different speeds. The Ancients called this great scale the Physical Plane.

A Plane meant a complete series or world of substances under one Law.

The Physical Plane includes solids, liquids, gases and the ethers of which we are told there are four. That totals up to seven 'states of matter', which go to make up the densest or chemical expression of life called the Physical Plane. We must remember that these 'states of matter' are mostly able to inter-penetrate each other, as we saw in Chapter 1.

The Physical Plane includes, of course, our Solar System, with its solids, gases and chemical rays.

Now, the Ancient Wisdom teaches that life is made up of Seven Planes or states of matter, of which the Physical Plane is only one—the densest or, in wireless parlance, the one of lowest frequency.

We are told that each of the Seven Major Planes is divided into seven sub-planes or strata, just as is the Physical Plane, each Plane and each Stratum being a mirror or counterpart of one of another series. Take the seven colours of the spectrum and split them up into seven shades of each colour, and you have a simile. Let the seven darkest shades represent the Physical Plane, and the seven palest and most luminous represent the Spiritual Plane. You will see how closely they are all connected with each other, even taking into account the complementary colours.

The Planes are neither above nor below one another, but interpenetrating, those which we think of as 'above' being of higher frequency from the standpoint of vibrations. (Bear in mind that all these things are very difficult to put into words.)

Everything in life, from a planet to a fly, from a cloud to a grain of sand, is interpenetrated by all these seven planes or worlds, and in most cases has a 'body' with which to function in each of them.

Man possesses a body made up of the material of the physical plane world, a body containing chemicals in liquid, solid and gaseous state. This body is interpenetrated by another body, which is its counterpart, and is made up of the four ethers. This is called his 'etheric' body, and constitutes a fine web through which the electric and radiating life-forces are fed into his physical body from the outer universe. This completes a man's physical plane equipment.

The next of the Seven Planes is called the Astral World. It is called by some the Desire World, as it is the sphere of emotions or desires. It contains the substance that stirs or motivates us. It is the world of attraction and repulsion.

Man has a body of this astral material, which is in full action when he is roused, excited, afraid, or full of desire—these feelings being, as we know, sometimes quite divorced from and stronger than our reasoning minds. It is possible for man, the individual, to separate his astral body from his physical body and wander about in it. Such an astral body can be seen by the astral eyes of another person, who will speak of it as a 'ghost'.

Everything physical has its counterpart in astral substance, so that a man wandering in his astral body can see chairs and tables, or, rather, their astral counterparts. The counterparts of physical things are made up of the lowest and densest stratum of the astral material, whereas the counterparts of thoughts and feelings are made up of the subtle and malleable kind of astral stuff. This has been described by clairvoyants as a moving and shimmering kaleidoscope of swiftly interchanging colours.

The Astral World is therefore almost impossible to visualize by anyone who has not been able to see it, but a vague idea of it can be obtained by a study of the various descriptions given to us by clairvoyants of all times.

The third of the Seven Great Planes is the world of thought or mind. The densest stratum of this Plane contains our own more worldly and material thoughts. The finer strata are used by cosmic intelligences for planning the architypes and activities of the universe. That is why if we can contact the higher strata of the mind-world or Mental Plane by training the corresponding parts of our brains (as all the sages have endeavoured to do), we shall gain inconceivable knowledge. The world of thought is even more difficult for us to picture than the Astral World, but as a beginning let us realize that it is said to interpenetrate all of life, like a sort of forceful 'gas'. It is not confined to the brain, which latter acts more like a kind of telephone switchboard to all the thoughts which pass through it.

The Fourth Plane is that of the Will or Life-spirit, and it is of this world that the *real* individual, the Ego, is a part. It is the Ego who uses the physical, astral and mind bodies as tools with which to achieve his purpose. When they are completely under his control and in harmony and balance one with another he becomes omnipotent and has achieved conquest over matter. He can, after careful training, shed his physical body like a coat and, leaving it safely in the nourishing care of its etheric web, continue his activities in his other bodies, or 'vehicles' as they are called.

When he wishes to return he slips back into the cramping and restricting burden which is his outer coating of flesh. We call this waking up, or returning to consciousness, as the case may be. He has often brought back useful knowledge which would benefit mankind, but the jar of contact once again with the heavy earth vibrations is so harsh that it usually snaps the thread of memory of the preceding activities, unless the person has been specially trained.

We have now come to a point where words are no longer even of the slightest help, so we will not attempt to describe the remaining three of the Seven Great Planes, those three which carry the consciousness through to a contact with the world of the Divine Creator Himself. It takes courage even to think, let alone speak, of such untranslatable wonders—but we do need such courage, and man is therefore obliged to reduce them to tiny Physical Plane conceptions able to be grasped by his five limited senses. Daring, however, is not without its reward, provided the motive is sincere, so man soon learns that he is more than an animal.

The Seven Planes, then, comprise the material of which the whole evolving universe is made. The Physical Plane, or solid world, takes up the smallest space, because it is condensed, and we can see it everywhere with our physical eyes. The etheric counterparts protrude an inch or two outside all living objects, and can be seen with the help of the Kilner glass screens.

The astral body protrudes to a still further extent, and is described by the clairvoyant who can tell a great deal about the individual by looking at it. Our earth also has an astral body, of course, which stretches very far out from its circumference. Incidentally, we shall have to accustom ourselves to the idea that the earth is a living creature, as are also the planets.

The Astral World is the world wherein the Fourth Dimension is to be found and understood. If you can imagine having eyes that see right through everything in all directions at once, you are visualizing your condition when functioning in the Astral World!

The thought-world, or Mental Plane, or that part of it which is the thought-body of our earth, extends still further outwards into interplanetary space. It presents a marvellous field of exploration for the mystic and the occultist.

The worlds of spirit occupy still larger space. The finest stratum of these, in the final world of Divine force, embraces all and flows uninterruptedly through everything. By this we can see what is meant when we are told that God, or Heaven, is within us. We are each able to contact the world of spirit within our own little bodies, because in the final analysis it is the life of that world which is interpenetrating and sustaining us.

We have taken but a superficial glance at the Law of the Seven Planes. It is open to us to reject or accept such a hypothesis, as we choose. But the exhaustive way in which all the workings of these Planes have been analysed gives us a most interesting and suggestive field of study, full of amazing and thrilling conceptions.

Let us summarize some of the main points once again.

According to this teaching, then, man has for his use first of all his solid physical body of low-frequency vibrations (an instrument or switchboard through which he contacts physical things).

Secondly, he owns a body of ether, interpenetrating this first body by reason of its higher and finer vibrations, and acting as an intermediary between it and the outer ether, a channel through which all the magnetic life-forces are fed to it.

Thirdly, he owns an 'astral' or 'ghost' body, interpenetrating the other two, and having much the same high speed of movement as electricity, at which speed he can travel when polarized entirely in the astral body (as in sleep).

Fourthly, there is his mental body, and well-known instances of thought telepathy travelling right across the world in the space of a few seconds prove to us the speed at which we can function while in this body. We often hear of cases of people appearing to their friends at the moment of their death, although living in a distant land.

Man's spiritual body is composed of the finest and most high-frequency vibrations of all, and can for that reason take control of all the lower ones. It can travel so fast that it can appear to be 'everywhere at once'. When man can consciously function in his spirit-body he is able finally to *conquer time and space, which only belong to a seventh part of the universe, the Physical Plane.*

It is very hard for present-day materially minded man to visualize these 'planes' and 'bodies'. But he must not allow his brain to remain inferior to that of the early races. The Egyptians, for instance, were quite at home with this knowledge, and drew and named the different 'bodies' of man on tombs and frescoes.

According to some authorities they symbolized them as follows:

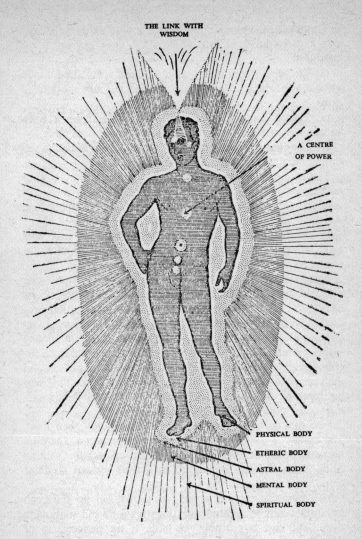

THE LINK WITH
WISDOM

A CENTRE
OF POWER

PHYSICAL BODY
ETHERIC BODY
ASTRAL BODY
MENTAL BODY
SPIRITUAL BODY

THE SEVEN BODIES OF MAN

They called the physical body KAT, a dead fish! The symbol was a curled-up dead fish, perhaps the most physical of all creatures.

(1) The etheric double was called KA, and symbolized, as the vehicle or holder of the body, by a breast and two upstretched arms.

(2) They called the astral body BA, symbolizing it by a human-headed bird, a bird being a 'traveller through space'.

(3) The spirit was represented by a lotus, which is able to rise out of the darkness and mud to reach the light.

The knowledge of these early peoples was astonishing. They understood so completely the power of mind over matter. One outstanding instance of this is seen in their feats of building, still incomprehensible to us.

It is said that they were able to wield the spirit-force over astral and physical substance and create entities to attach to the tombs, to guard them for centuries.

Present-day scientists are busy exploding the atom with magnetic and electric force, but so far the results of their efforts have been dubious, because of the poisonous by-products produced.[1] Perhaps they are doing things the wrong way round, using physical-plane instruments of low vibrations to try to control higher vibrations. They might do better if they could train the only high-powered instrument they possess—the mind—as did the ancient scientists. The true alchemists tried to use the burning force of the concentrated mind as the crucible in which they could distil the elixir of life from gold.

Fire can burn up anything of lower vibration than itself. The mind can control fire, being of higher vibration. There are many authentic cases of people who can contact fire without being burnt and can be pierced by knives without shedding blood.

The mind can act very quickly on matter, but the spirit can act instantaneously, rearranging the vibrations and re-forming them. This fact is probably the basis of the performance of 'miracles' and 'faith-healing'.

[1] *The Secret of the Atomic Age*, by the same author.

Many people are testing these things out, through mesmerism, hypnotism, thought-reading, psychometry, and other methods.

The explorer along such lines will find that the etheric body has been weighed by scientists; that the aura can be seen through a glass prepared by psychic researchers; that numberless people have had experience of the astral body; that the vibrations of the mental body have been recorded by instruments; and the power of the spirit-body demonstrated by innumerable 'miracles'.

It is natural to be sceptical about many of these things, but he who is wise will keep an open mind until he has fairly tested the various proofs available to him.

5

HOW WE ARE CLASSIFIED

WE ARE told that the attainment of wisdom and power can only be acquired through study and knowledge of ourselves. We have seen also that the same laws govern the whole universe, and that if man can understand some of the laws governing himself or the tiniest atom he will have a clue to those which govern the solar systems and the greater system to which they belong. Scientists have discovered that an atom closely resembles a miniature solar system. This leads us to the thought that perhaps our great solar system in its turn is one of millions of atoms forming the body of some great Being too vast for us to picture. Such a Being might feel small compared to the world which He in turn finds surrounding Himself.

Let us carry this idea a little further. The atoms (the stars) forming the cells (constellations) of the body of this vast Being would not appear to be far apart to Him; seen by Him they would be intimately connected with each other, there being strong chemical reactions and influences between them, just as with the cells in our own bodies. When an atom from one of our own cells is examined it is found to be composed of a proton (or sun) surrounded by various numbers of electrons (or planets) all vibrating at set speeds. Now, we are told that the proton is so small a part of the atom that it can be compared with a bee buzzing inside a cathedral! So that if we could become small enough to cling to that proton we should certainly feel as if we were clinging to a star in a mighty space, and it would be difficult to believe that our star was part of an atom in the cell of a very solid body!

Some scientists now claim that the ether itself is denser than the planets that swing through it, so you see we must reserve ideas about solidity until we are a little better informed.

The point made in this case is that through visualizing our vast giant we can better understand the intimate relation in which the stars stand to each other. Composed of chemicals held together by force or energy, the radiations from each star and planet strongly affect each other, carrying with them chemicals in a very fine and subtle form. Thus from the planet Mercury we should expect to receive rays of the wave-length that belongs to Mercury, and containing mercury itself in a fine form; also certain other chemicals which are contained in the planet to a lesser degree. As our solar system is believed to have been formed from the splitting up of one star, every planet, every man and every atom within it must still be held and connected one with another by the interplay of identical chemical radiations. As an example, it is said that a ruby is actually a fragment of that part of the original star which finally broke away to form the planet Mars.

The astrologer makes careful calculations of the chemical and spiritual influences set up by the continual changing of the relative positions of the planets and luminaries (sun and moon), and of their effect upon the microcosm or tiny replica which is man. The macro-microcosmic law comes into play also in the question of time. A man's whole life is said to be mirrored in the moment of his birth.

According to one school of astrologists a person's individuality, his positive side, his character, are determined by the zodiacal sign in which the sun is found at his birth. His personality, or negative side, is determined by the sign in which the moon is found at his birth. When he is born he is 'tuned in', as it were, to the play of the planetary influences at the time, and the vibrations set up within him rule him all his life, determining his reactions both chemical and characteristic, and the environment which they attract.

It is in this way that people are classified.

There are at present scientific experiments in progress whose object is to indicate the differing results of inaugurating the same chemical mixtures at various phases of the planets, and also the different reactions at such times in plants and animals.

The ancient sages had a great knowledge of this fascinating subject and considered it of paramount importance. First of all they conducted endless studies about the planets, and we call the results of their research Astronomy. They next made extraordinarily complicated and exhaustive studies of the combined influences of the planets on both the earth and human beings, according to their different positions in the heavens at various times. The results of this particular research have come down to us embodied in another science which we call astrology.

Astrology divides the heavens into twelve portions, rather like the divisions of an orange. These divisions, called the Twelve Signs of the Zodiac, correspond roughly with the twelve months of the year. Each of these Signs is governed by one of the planets. According to the month of the year in which you were born you can tell which Sign rules your life, and consequently what sort of health you may expect to enjoy, and what your characteristics will be.

Astrology is such a lengthy study and so difficult a science that there are few really expert astrologers in the world. Those few who do exist usually belong to a family of astrologers, whose teaching has been handed down for generations. A genuine astrologer must make complete calculations of the interplay of influences, chemical and otherwise, of every planet upon the person or subject under consideration.

But anyone can make a beginning with a simple study of the Twelve Signs of the Zodiac, and although the information gained is only generalization, it is close to the truth and therefore helpful and can be used by those who have not learnt to cast a horoscope.

To attain his final development, man is supposed to be born under the Signs of the Zodiac one by one, to learn the lessons they teach. Sometimes he is obliged to learn one of these lessons for the third time, perhaps for the thirtieth!

This has all been beautifully expressed in the *Twelve Labours of Hercules*, which was written with a profound knowledge of both astrology and symbolism, and contains deeply occult meaning.

The ancients declared that the whole history of the evolution of mankind, the solar system, and the universe is described and foretold by the stars, grouped in a kind of mystic shorthand, and capable of perfect translation. Such translations are contained in many of the hidden archives.

In respect of our year, one Sign of the Zodiac, with its planet, is ruling from about the 21st to the 21st of each month.

The influences of the Signs overlap each other slightly, so that a person born between about the 15th to the 25th of the month is influenced by two Signs (being born near to their junction). This gives him a more complex character. The most composite influence takes place on the 22nd of the month, so we find many prominent characters born on that date, such as Wagner, Van Dyck, Byron, Bacon, George Washington, Hitler, Conan Doyle, Baden-Powell, Faraday, and Rider Haggard.

A person born during the first half of the month comes under the unmixed influence of the sign, and would therefore be of a more definite type.

It must be understood, however, that in dividing the whole of humanity into only twelve types we are merely taking the first step. We are only generalizing, and although we have made an important beginning we must not take it as the final word.

The birth of Christ took place at a rare and wonderful conjunction of the stars, by which they announced (in the aforementioned shorthand) that tremendous event.

The Three Wise Men, who were Astrologer Kings of Chaldea, had been waiting for this conjunction to occur, and when they saw its approach they set off to journey to Jerusalem, over which town it was apparent that it would take place. They arrived and told King Herod, who at once realized the significance of the conjunction, which heralded a new 'King'. Herod called all his wise astrologers together and 'inquired of them diligently what time the star appeared'. They were all much troubled.

History is full of stories illustrating the immense importance given to astrology, of which astronomy was but the foundation. All priests and governors in olden days had to be well versed in the science of the stars and in the science of numbers, and we find that this knowledge existed all over the then known world.

We have only time here to take a superficial glance at the way in which we can apply astrology to the understanding of ourselves, and also of racial and world conditions.

By means of this science it is considered possible to map out the whole of a person's life. This is done in the first place by using the law 'As in the Microcosm so in the Macrocosm', and therefore by postulating that the plan of a person's threescore years is mirrored in the first day, and even in the first moments, of his life. In the same way the history of a race or country can be determined by the influences under which it had its inception.

These things can, of course, only be believed through the study of proofs. The way to obtain these proofs is first of all to study astrology (!) and then to consider the hundreds of horoscopes of famous people which are available, as well as the annals of history itself.

In Astrology the great law of cause and effect (Karma) plays a big part. If, for instance, a man is greedy, it is not magical to predict that at a future date he will suffer from a digestive trouble, or if he is rash and impetuous that an accident is very sure to befall him. The average astrologer will predict the accident, but if instead he would study the cause, and persuade the man to cure his rashness, Karma would be defeated or adjusted, and the accident need not happen. 'The wise man is master of his stars, the fool is ruled by them.'

A conscientious astrologer always tries to show a person what tendencies he has to master, instead of playing upon his love of sensation by describing future events. What does a man need with his future before he has any idea of how to deal with the present? Today contains all possibilities for those who know how to strive for them.

Astrology has been sadly neglected as a science, but lately it is beginning to come into its own again, under the patient research-work of hard-headed scientists who are quite unsuspecting of that which they are about to unearth.

One of the principal uses to which Astrology can be put is

the thorough diagnosis of a patient, bringing to light the chemical deficiencies or maladjustments in his internal laboratory, and the planetary rays which he is able to assimilate and use, or those which are causing him trouble. This method will do away with all guesswork, it is claimed, as we are assured that it is an exact science and will play a large part in the future of medicine.

Some of the biochemical experts have declared that the twelve principal cell-salts found in the human body are ruled by the twelve Signs of the Zodiac. They affirm that a person uses up more of the cell-salt belonging to the Sign under which he was born, as that chemical is connected with the key-note of his activity. Therefore the first deficiency that occurs in his internal laboratory is this cell-salt, his 'birth salt', and the various symptoms of his ills may be traced primarily to this depletion. All this was apparently known to the ancients, but as they gave to the cell-salts the names of gods, and described their activities in mythical parables, we are only just beginning to understand what they meant.

Let us now take a rapid glance at the major general classifications of astrological characteristics:

The Twelve Signs of the Zodiac represent the twelve lessons of human existence, the twelve qualities to be developed in the formation of the perfect man. It is said that these qualities are gradually achieved by every human being, life after life, but not necessarily Sign after Sign. That is where man's free-will comes in. If he chooses to work under some particular Sign more often than the others, or repulses the lesson of one Sign altogether, a one-sided character results, such as a genius with evil tendencies.

The Zodiacal year begins at the vernal equinox on March 21st, with the Sign of Aries. The symbol of Aries is a Ram, because the ram pushes his head into the wintry stubble and ploughs it up with his horns to expose the new budding green upon which his family can feed. Aries represents the first crude uprush of life, the beginning of the human journey, and therefore bestows extreme physical activity, daring and impulsiveness upon its natives. Aries rules the head, and therefore the Arian, or person born between March 21st and April 21st, uses the brain intensively, although without much experience of life to back him. Aries is ruled by Mars, the warlike planet. So man, at the beginning of his journey, spoils for a fight, is a born leader, eager, brave, with quick-working brain. Keen to help, he is a poor judge of character, and often deceived. He makes a bad sub-

ordinate, and although plucky, he is full of fears, because he has not yet developed much faith or philosophy. These Arians should be guarded from overworking the brain and given plenty of sleep. Hans Christian Andersen was an Aries born, although a very advanced type.

From April 21st to May 21st we have the second Sign, that of

Taurus. Its symbol is a bull, and those born under it partake of the nature of that animal. They are very strong but quiet and plodding, until, if suddenly roused, they plunge ruthlessly to their goal. They are ruled by the planet Venus, and so love is a part of man's second lesson; he can love devotedly and work the earth patiently. It is among the Taurians that we find many of our great agriculturists and lovers of nature, also our singers and poets. Often they serve their fellow-men with courage and devotion. Sir James Barrie and Florence Nightingale are examples of this Sign.

Taurus folk are very strong, and easily over-nourished. Their chief ills arise from too-luxurious living.

Having learnt both activity and service the next lesson which man has to tackle is how to use the brain for practical matters and for reasoning. This is the work of those born under the third Sign, Gemini, May 21st to June 21st, whose symbol is 'The Twins'. This symbol represents a dual type of mind, one who can see both sides of a question, and jumps with keen interest to every new idea presented. Such people, apparently changeable and ambitious (without knowing exactly for what), and whose brains race like chattering birds from branch to branch of the tree of knowledge, have difficult characters to govern. They are ruled by the planet Mercury, which gives quickness and brilliance, and through an intensive study of life they learn to develop a logical reasoning mind. This brilliance and rapidity of thought depends upon the nervous system more than on the brain, so these people must be guarded against overworking their nerves.

Advanced types will have attained to a very broad vision, and we can take as examples Elgar and Dean Inge.

Our human being has by now gained much experience, and so his next lesson is to learn how to apply it. The fourth Sign, Cancer, June 21st to July 22nd, bestows great patience and tenacity, and a genius for parenthood and family life. As we develop, however, we of course become more complex, and so Cancer people are sometimes restless and love to travel. The symbol of Cancer is the Crab, who carries his house on his back, and moves through life in a curious zig-zag way, suddenly going backwards again when least expected. Cancer people are like that. Just when about to achieve success they will turn back, or begin something else, and so in spite of their industry they have a life of ups and downs. Sir Joshua Reynolds ruined many of his pictures through continually changing his method of painting. Cancer people are ruled by the Moon, which makes them deeply sensitive and passionate. They badly need a life of discipline and order.

Henry VIII is a good example of a Cancer type who became undisciplined, and John Calvin of one who went to the other extreme.

Now we come to the point where man has learnt a great deal of the human side of life and is able to produce very fine results. His next task, therefore, is to stand forth as a powerful and well-developed human being, capable of high achievements.

The fifth Sign is Leo the Lion, July 22nd to August 23rd. We sometimes find born under it the kings of men—people of power, large-hearted, strong both mentally and physically, proud, ambitious and popular. They have not yet touched the Divine Intuition, and so as a rule they misunderstand and despise those weaker than themselves, although they attract many sycophants. They often suffer cruel disillusion in their friendships, through their own inadaptability. They are ruled by the Sun (the heart of the solar system) and are therefore liable to high blood-pressure and other affections of the heart and circulation.

We expect to find famous people born under this Sign, and sure enough among them are Napoleon, Mussolini and H. P. Blavatsky.

Having risen to great heights through impulsiveness, forceful-ness and the talent for self-expression, the next quality to be acquired is that of discrimination, of taste, the lack of which brought Leo into many unhappy relationships. Therefore we find that the sixth Sign, Virgo, August 23rd to September 23rd, whose symbol is the Virgin, teaches this lesson.

Virgo people are born with a natural fastidiousness and critical faculty. They are ruled by Mercury, who also held sway over the people of Gemini, but whereas in that Sign great energy was expended in the collecting of facts from all quarters, the Virgo people have all that experience to draw upon, plus the fruit garnered in Cancer and Leo. So they are able to take up life from the angle of the critic rather than the man of action. They are adaptable to almost any pursuit, make excellent subordinates, are plodding, and generally successful. Their exquisite taste is evident in many walks of life. From their ranks are drawn both restaurant-keepers and art critics! Journalism and hygiene also attract them.

They rely on the material side of life, and because Mercury rules the nerves they often suffer from ills due to worry, hypersensitiveness and imagination. Nevertheless, they can be controlled, practical and resourceful. We can study one of the higher types of the Sign in Elizabeth, the Virgo or Virgin Queen.

The Sign of Virgo ends at the autumnal equinox on September 23rd, so we have therefore traversed the first half of man's journey round the Zodiac. He has learnt how to be the complete human being; but yet only half his journey is accomplished! The remaining half will be taken up in learning to give over the reins of power to the spiritual man, and live in both worlds at once, with feet firmly planted on the earth, but with mind in communion with the Divine. The man has now become the aspirant, realizing that there is a world for his conquering worth infinitely more than the physical world. His task now becomes harder to understand, but the first thing that such a man must achieve is *balance*. And so the symbol of Libra, September 23rd to October 23rd, the seventh Sign, is the Balance.

The Libran seeks balance all through his life. In fact, he misses many opportunities through too much weighing and balancing in his mind—through 'second thoughts'! In his case these are not always the wisest. He has reached the stage where man is becoming psychic and intuitive, and he would do well to act on his first impressions. Librans are ruled by Venus, and so are full of love, but their love has become more mental than physical. They are able to love abstract things such as harmony. justice and beauty, and they shrink from all disharmonies in life,

Some of them will do anything to avoid a row. This desire for harmony and balance deprives them of the more direct energy and impulsiveness of the preceding Signs. The refining process has begun, but those who do not understand may think Librans cowardly and weak. They may sometimes be condemned to rather colourless lives. We find among their ranks many lawyers, judges and specialists, also architects and research-workers, as all these require the qualities of care and balance. Their personal life is often unhappy, through their being too analytical of other people and afraid to let themselves go. So we can be sure that they must guard against loneliness and depression, which feelings often cause them to overwork themselves.

As examples of the advanced types of Librans we can take Faraday, Sarah Bernhardt and Annie Besant.

Having begun to learn how to transmute the tender passion of love to higher planes, man's next step is to bend the warlike force of Mars in the same direction. So we see that the eighth Sign, Scorpio, October 23rd to November 22nd, is ruled by Mars, giving to its natives a strong, forceful and magnetic personality. We are coming now to the types who are so stored with accumulated magnetism and experience, so full of 'character' that they exercise great fascination, and sometimes call forth fanatical devotion from their friends.

The Sign of Scorpio has produced more saints than almost any other, and probably more villains too. These people are capable of the best or the worst, but never of being negative or unnoticed. Therefore, Scorpio has three symbols, firstly the scorpion—the animal who bites itself with its tail, representing the man who is his own enemy; secondly, the Serpent, representing the birth of wisdom, and thirdly, the White Eagle soaring to the sun, showing the final rising upwards from earthly ties and attaining the spiritual sunlight. The Scorpio native usually passes through the fire of the temptation of sex in all its forms. He has to learn that it is his sex-force which he needs for use in higher channels, and no other. He is usually versatile, full of ideas, a leader who can sway audiences, a mental fighter, proud, ambitious, sensitive and a good organizer. He is capable of intense and enduring feelings. The higher types are the humanitarians, peacemakers and philosophers.

The Scorpio native should be guarded against evil companions and always allowed to wield authority. We can take as examples Saint Augustine, Mahomet, Martin Luther and Edward VII.

By this time man has become a very potential being, though still extremely self-centred. The 'I' dominates everything. So that in the next stage of development we find the beginnings of un-selfishness taking shape. The ninth Sign is that of Saggitarius, November 22nd to December 21st. Its symbol is the archer shooting straight into the sky, representing the quick, strong mind leaping at its goal, Truth. These people instinctively grasp the fact that Truth is beautiful and joyful, and translate that realization into a keen wish to spread joy and beauty around them. They are the lovers of life, full of kindly humour. They may be domineering, egotistical and stubborn; but they cannot live without attempting to make their companions happy. They are therefore usually the souls of hospitality. They give great encouragement to music, the arts, and all the pleasures and luxuries of life. Containing as they do the qualities of all pre-ceding signs, they are extremely versatile, but as they are ruled by Jupiter, music and ceremonial make a special appeal to them. Their love of life makes them an easy prey to self-indulgence, and they are very excitable and emotional.

Most of their ills come from these two characteristics. Their agile minds and prophetic instinct cause them to jump to results without patient study, and this is a snare to their undoing. They often fail to appreciate the worth of slower folk.

As they are high-powered people, Saggitarians must always be actively employed, but they should have short intervals of complete rest in which to relax their tenseness. Because of their zest for life they are very popular. We can take as examples Lord Beaconsfield, Queen Alexandra, Heine and Winston Churchill.

We have arrived at the stage where man has at last realized the wonder of spiritual accomplishment, and has bent his will to attain it. His challenge is at once accepted, and Saturn or Satan, the great tester and trainer of humanity, steps in to help.

So we find that the tenth Sign, Capricorn, December 21st to January 21st, is ruled by the planet Saturn, whose metal is lead, and who exerts a heavy crushing influence, holding his victim down to earth, pressing and pressing upon him until all the dross in his nature is forced out.

The symbol of Capricorn is the Goat. Man has ceased to be the sheep, listening and following others' lead; he has decided to stand on his own feet and work out his own salvation. He wants proof of all that he may hitherto have believed. So the Capricornian is, above all, thoughtful and practical, outwardly perhaps a materialist, yet with a worship of intellect and an interest in the sciences and in the occult. He is independent, proud and domineering, happiest when leading and organizing. Although he lacks the kindly humour of Saggitarius and the brilliant enthusiasm of Leo, he has more tact, pity and patience than either, and with these he is beginning to earn his Godhead. He is learning to see outside of himself, using his own sufferings to identify himself with the feelings of all humanity. Such a one is likely to become a Communist, a Socialist, or fighter for some ideal. The difficult personal adjustments he is making often cause him to be hard to understand, complex and peculiar in some of his reactions. Nevertheless, in spite of the stern discipline of his life he is usually long-lived and rarely is obliged to call in the doctor.

We can take as examples of the higher types Joan of Arc, Woodrow Wilson, Benjamin Franklin and Gladstone.

Saturn's intensive work on man is not completed by the end of the Sign of Capricorn, so he carries it right through the next Zodiacal month. The Sign of Aquarius, January 21st to February 21st, which follows, is also ruled by that planet. By now, man has lost much of his crudity, and having had some of his pride knocked out of him, he is less egocentric. He feels that he is a part of the Whole, and has made a great step forward in that he is beginning to give more importance to others than to himself. The Symbol of Aquarius is the Water-Carrier pouring out the Waters of Life upon mankind and the child of this Sign loves to merge himself with people, in gatherings and functions; he

loves to work in intimate relation with the masses. He is vision-
ary and inventive and has a great desire for the public welfare.
No longer ambitious for the self, he is apt to remain in the background unless inspired to work for a cause, in which case he can
rise to great heights and can then push forward quite imperson-
ally. The Aquarian mind is learning to be non-attached, clear-
cut, honest, with a love of freedom, and a sympathy with human
weakness. He is still over-sensitive. He reads character instinctively, 'seeing through' people, and this gives him intense likes
and dislikes. He has already developed some of the finer subtle
qualities of the soul, and this causes him to be very delicately
balanced. For this reason he often feels frail in health, although
in reality he has great reserve force.

As examples of the higher types we can take Abraham Lincoln,
Charles Dickens, Swedenborg, Darwin, Ruskin and Voltaire.

The merging of the self into other peoples' lives produces
genius for the stage, so we also find such people as Nell Gwynne,
Pavlova and Sir Henry Irving under Aquarius.

We have now arrived at the last Sign of the twelve, the one
therefore under which the most perfected type of spiritual man
can be born. This Sign is called Pisces and lasts from February 21st to March 21st. Its symbol is the Fish, which is also the
symbol of Christianity. The lesson of Pisces is a final letting go
of the self, the complete merging into the lives and feelings of
others. Therefore under this Sign are born our most brilliant
actors. The inspiration which the people of Pisces have earned
produces also fine poets, dramatists and musicians. The strongest
and the weakest types are born at this time. The force which
flows through the Piscean is difficult to handle, and unless he
turns it to good account it may drive him to drugs, drink and
other excesses. The Sign is a dual one, so the two Ways are open.
The native may rise, if inspired, to any heights of self-denial
and attainment, but he needs encouragement and confidence in
himself. As with all the later Signs, his character is complex and
versatile. His past training gives him a 'natural' understanding;
he absorbs knowledge rather than studies it. Pisces is ruled by
Jupiter, who bestows brilliance and a love of ceremony, as we

saw in Saggitarius. So our Piscean contributes much to the decorative and romantic in life, and this arouses intense and sometimes fanatical devotion in his friends. If these friends push him in the right way he can become a great public servant, but he depends upon co-operation with others—he prefers to work in brotherhood. He has identified himself with the universe, and this gives him a great love of travel and the sea.

From the advanced types in this Sign we can choose Chopin, Michael Angelo, David Livingstone, David Garrick and Ibsen.

We have now completed our initial review of the types born under the twelve Signs. We must, however, remember that astrology subdivides them *ad infinitum*, and that the laws of rebirth, Karma and free-will arrange for numberless variations of the order in which people progress through these Signs. The number of times they have accomplished the full round will determine whether they are 'old and experienced souls' or 'new souls'. The old souls are of course becoming more rounded out as they approach the state of perfect man, who is a blend of the best in all the Signs. The examples which we have given of famous people are therefore the older souls, and not really very typical of their Sign, but the mediocre and simple types rarely leave their mark in history.

With regard to the twelve cell-salts which are the principal agents of activity in the human body, let us note the interesting relation they are said to bear to the Signs of the Zodiac.[1]

Aries, the Ram, the brain worker, uses up very much of the Potassium Phosphate which nourishes the brain fluid and produces the highest rate of vibration in the body. A deficiency causes brain-fag and lack of comprehension.

Taurus, the Bull, ruling the liver, governs the cell-salt Sulphate of Sodium, which eliminates excess water from the body, due to the abundant intake of the luxury-loving Taurian. A deficiency of this salt causes such ills as diabetes and quinsy.

Gemini, the Twins, ruling the nervous system, governs that cell-salt Potassium Chloride, which forms fibrin in the blood and

[1] See *The Zodiac and the Salts of Salvation*, by G. W. Carey and I. E. Perry.

so builds the nerves; while a deficiency causes thickening of the fibrin, and therefore bronchitis, asthma and other nervous diseases result.

Cancer, the tenacious Crab, rules the spleen, and governs the salt Fluoride of Lime, which builds the tenacious elastic fibres holding the body together. A deficiency of this causes sagging throughout the organs, with many attendant ills, from depression to dropsy.

Leo, the Sun, ruler of the heart and vitality, governs the salt Phosphate of Magnesia, which regulates the muscular spasms such as those controlling the heart-beats. A deficiency causes cramps, lack of muscular force, palpitations and meningitis.

Virgo, ruler of the solar plexus and stomach, governs the salt Potassium Sulphate, which makes the oil necessary to keep the machinery going throughout the body. A deficiency causes thickening of the oil, which clogs the pores and produces various forms of stagnation.

Libra, the Balance, ruler of the kidneys, governs the cell-salt Carbonate of Sodium. This salt holds the balance between the acids and the fluids in the system, and produces harmonious life. A deficiency engenders acidity, with hate, jealousy, depression and their attendant ailments, such as headache and lumbago.

Scorpio, the Scorpion, ruler of the sex organs, governs the cell-salt Sulphate of Lime. This needs to be transmuted by water to form the white plaster of Paris; this strengthens the whole system and gives tone to the grey matter of the brain. A deficiency demoralizes the brain, destroying the power of elevated thought, and renders the body prone to infectious diseases.

Saggitarius, the archer, rules the thighs, and governs the cell-salt Silica, which is really quartz. This is formed of strong minute *arrow*-shaped pieces, which stiffen the walls of hair, nails, nerve sheaths and cells, and pierce a way outwards to the surface for necessary eruptions. A deficiency produces weakness of the cell-walls, leading to various forms of self-poisoning such as rheumatism and other inflammations.

Capricorn, the Goat, rules the bones, and governs the cell-salt Calcium-Phosphate. This uses albumen to make cement for bones. A deficiency causes diseases due to overflow of albumin, which upsets the gastric juices and brings on such inflictions as Bright's Disease and other digestive troubles.

Aquarius, the Water-Carrier, rules the white corpuscles, and governs the cell-salt Sodium Chloride, which acts as *water-carrier* to the human system. A deficiency causes general frailty and such diseases as jaundice.

Pisces, the Fish, rules the feet, the foundation of the body, and the red corpuscles, and governs the cell-salt Phosphate of Iron, which is the foundation of the blood. A deficiency gives bad circulation, chills and fevers.

Here, then, we have a rough idea as to how the planetary rays are said to affect the chemicals within us and our own reactions. Much research work along these lines by certain of the bio-chemists and other scientists is in progress at present. Naturally the reactions of the cell-salts overlap and interplay with great complexity, and the science would appear to be a deep one.

How much truth there is in all this, and how much study it would take to produce useful results, are questions which we must leave to the student who feels disposed to investigate.

We cannot leave this science of Astrology without applying the Micro-Macrocosmic Law to it, and observing how it works out on a larger scale. According to its findings, then, our own sun with its planets is in its turn revolving round a parent sun. The Signs of the Zodiac repeat themselves in a still greater cycle, during which our sun takes about 2500 years to pass through each Sign, but as this greater movement is in the opposite direc-tion from the smaller one, the Signs follow one another in reverse order. Each of these great periods is called an 'Age'. During 2000 years of the Jewish Dispensation the sun was pass-ing through Aries, the Ram, which animal figures very largely in sacrifice and symbol of the time.

Before that Period there was the Age of Taurus, wherein the winged bull (representing the Taurian capacity for rising to spiritual heights) was worshipped and sculptured by such people as the Chaldeans and Assyrians.

The Sphinx would appear, in this light, to have been built

during the Age of Leo, somewhere before 10,000 B.C., as it has a lion's body.

Following the Jewish came the Christian Dispensation, under the Sign of Pisces, the Fish. The fish is the symbol of Christianity, and some of us are required to eat it every Friday. The 2000 years of the Piscean Age drew to a close with the nineteenth century, and we are now coming gradually into the new Age. This is the Aquarian Age, when the 'waters of life will be poured out to all mankind'. During this period we are told that Universal Brotherhood will become an accomplished fact and a Golden Age will be brought to birth.

According to these calculations, then, it must be about 34,000 years since the previous Aquarian Period, containing also a Golden Age. Historians who study this particular question proclaim that this took place on the lost continent of Atlantis, whose submergence caused the spread of its culture to other lands.

There have been several hundred books written on Atlantis, many founded on geological and biological research.

The subject is one which is apt to stir racial memory and enlarge man's viewpoint. It enables him to understand the inevitable succession of cycles and therefore to prepare hopefully at this time for the Golden Age which is promised to us soon by the shorthand in the skies.

6

MALE AND FEMALE

LET us see what part the much-tormented question of Sex plays in this deeper conception of life that we are trying to reach.

We must follow our usual procedure and first try to get at the roots and underlying causes, taking as broad and as scientific a view of the subject as we can.

We find that male and female are really the positive and negative aspects in nature—that is to say, that male is the positive or electrical quality and female is the magnetic, receptive or negative quality. When the two fuse, creative action occurs. The word 'negative' is here used in its electrical application, and means that which does not act but holds power. It does not represent futility or weakness, but reserve force.

The whole of the universe is built upon this fusion of 'male' and 'female'. From the greatest planet to the tiniest chemical cell the same process goes on. It is really as if the world were an electric pole containing vast numbers of other electric poles of all sizes down to the most minute. Let us consider this question of electricity for a moment. Quite simply, you have a current of electricity passing down a 'pole' or straight line—the pole can be a bar of iron, a planet or a person; one side of the pole is the 'positive' or electrical side, and the other side is the 'negative' or magnetic side.

The magnetic side draws to itself, absorbs and retains power. When it contacts the positive—i.e. the action, or electrical—side of the pole, it gives off this power, combustion occurs, a spark is lit, and force is *generated*. It is exactly this process which causes a planet to rotate, moves a car, creates a child, or makes a plant grow.

The positive electrical male side of nature is represented by the acids, and the passive female magnetic side of nature is represented by the alkalis. Before a planet or a car moves, the right constituents of acid and alkali must be assembled, to create the little explosions of electrical life-force which brings action about. It is also this identical driving-force which motivates our bodies. The tiniest cell in our bodies is an electric battery in a state of combustion; just as our whole body is also electrically polarized.

The acid part of our bodies is the action part, the muscles; the alkali part of us is the blood, which holds and carries the power to those muscles. When in a state of health the two are rightly balanced, but at death the power which holds them apart (the pole) is withdrawn and the acid floods the alkaline blood, causing the whole mechanism to become static.

In chemistry you must take an alkali element and combine it with an acid element if you want to create a compound which is strong and useful. If you want to make a bomb (which is only condensing the production of force into a small space) you must also bring together an acid and an alkali—when they are allowed to meet the bomb explodes.

The same thing happens when a well-matched man and woman meet—attraction leads to combination and then action!

It must not be inferred, however, that a man is all electrical and a woman all magnetic. On the contrary, these two qualities run in juxtaposition through every cell and atom. But all existing things are pre-eminently of one sex, although containing both interiorly in various degrees. The planet Mars, for instance, is pre-eminently masculine, but of course is held in manifestation by its pole of positive and negative. Our earth has its pole running through it, called North and South at its two ends, and, of course, one side of the earth is electrical and the other magnetic.

So also a man and a woman, though pre-eminently male-electric and female-magnetic, have each what we might call their poles running through them. The right side of our bodies is electric and the left side magnetic—the right side the side of action and the left the female or heart side.

The subdivision of these two continues to infinity in our

bodies, until each tiny cell has its pole, and even each atom, as we know, is revolving round its pole or axis.

Thus throughout the whole of life from the greatest to the tiniest we have the same process going on. The female magnetic power attracts the male electric force and creation and action takes place.

Now, as this process runs throughout everything we may expect to find an expression of it in our own brain, and we do! The human brain has a shape curiously like the human embryo, and it contains a part which is male and a part which is female. When these two parts are co-ordinated by mental training and concentration, and made to co-operate, a most wonderful development takes place, and the mind becomes inspired, forceful and creative.

This was well known to the very ancient peoples. In their own remarkable way they worshipped the means by which a human being can contact 'God' within his own brain. They worshipped those symbols of the male-female power in the head.

Succeeding generations, in their ignorance, debased this worship into the Phallic worship of sex in its physical sense. Our ideas about the things that matter have grown smaller and smaller down the centuries, until at present they are almost non-existent!

We can now begin to glimpse the truths lying behind the worship, in many ancient civilizations, of the great Trinities of Life. The Christians adopted them, and gave us God (the Life-force), the Virgin or Mother (the wisdom or stored power), and the Son, the result of that blending, the One who *acts* and achieves. In most ancient religions we can trace an appreciation of this Trinity.

The alchemists expressed the Triangle in their own way, as Mercury, Sulphur, and Salt (our cell-salts being that which builds and acts within our own bodies).

Then there is also our Sun, the male electrical positive force whose rays strike the magnetic female Moon; the combination of both rays reaching the earth causes fertilization, movement and growth.

For a long time we have been accustomed in our little limited way to think of sex only in the primitive terms of our power of physical procreation, not as the vast process on which the whole universe is built. Infinitely petty and restricting taboos have shamefacedly locked up the entire question in a secret box in our minds. We muddle along in complete ignorance, oblivious that the box contains our greatest jewels.

Let us now take out these jewels of ours and study their value.

We are confronted throughout history with certain symbols. One of them is the serpent, which was always much in evidence wherever the ancient temples devoted to wisdom flourished. Since the old story of Adam and Eve, the serpent has represented two things—Knowledge and Sex—thus hinting at a close connection between them. And the secret is that the Creative Force within us is one single force, whether it be used for physical or mental ends. We have the choice as to which way we shall direct this force, upwards or downwards.

In material-minded or primitive man it continues to be used purely for procreation or sensual gratification. But as man aspires to higher ideals, as he yearns to create mentally and live in the spirit, the force is gradually drawn upwards to the creative principles in the brain.

This force is called by the Easterns the Kundalini, and is likened to a serpent of fire lying coiled at the base of the spine. If man steadily purifies his mind and nature through living chastely and moderately, he is able to magnetize the Kundalini serpent upwards through the channel of his spine, until finally it reaches the Masculine-Feminine principles of the brain and fires them into co-ordination. The man is then filled with inspiration and becomes attuned to the inner world of Wisdom. This can only be accomplished with the help of the 'Kundalini serpent'. Perhaps Christ gave a hint of this when He said: 'Be ye wise as serpents.'

Men and women have, therefore, the choice as to what they will do with this power within them. Shall they exhaust it in the various self-indulgencies of sex-life, both mental and physical, or shall they use it to become creative in the realms of the spirit and higher mind—a force for good? It is this tremendous choice

which every human being has to face. Usually they face it unconsciously or in the dark, because of the utter helplessness of
present-day education in these matters. Hardly one of the many
pitfalls surrounding them is properly explained.

It is easy to convince ourselves of the fact that it is one and
the same force which feeds either the procreative organs or the
brain. The gland specialists have brought much to light proving
this. They tell us that the Pineal Gland in the head acts as a brake
upon sex development. As we have said, it was once a third eye.
Now it regulates the action of light upon the body. If it is diseased
or inactive we get precocious sex-development. The Pituitary
Body, in the head, is the gland of intellectuality, promoting the
mathematical and artistic powers. When it is deficient sexual
abnormalities result.

We also have the evidence of our numberless lunatic asylums,
peopled largely with those whose brains have deteriorated
through sex excesses of various kinds.

On the other hand we have many cases of people who apparently have gone mad as the result of fanatical piousness.

This needs another explanation. Here we have come up
against the result of what might be termed SPIRITUAL GREED.
A person who is greedy and self-indulgent on the physical plane
will naturally not change his character just because he decides
that more benefit will accrue from a pursuit of spiritual assets.
It is possible to be greedy for spiritual food which is as yet un-
deserved. Very often people attempt to make in a few years the
spiritual progress for which they should have been patiently
working all their lives. The result is that the body has not had
time for its vibrations to become purified and raised to a higher
tempo, and the brain is still full of the dregs of worldly and
impure thoughts. When, therefore, by a forcing process, the
Kundalini serpent of fire is prematurely driven up the spine,
burning away all dross as it goes, and it arrives within a brain
unfitted to receive it, parts of the brain cannot stand this bath
of fire and perish with the sudden burning of the dross they still
contain, and various forms of derangement ensue.

Many highly dangerous breathing exercises originating in the

East are designed with the purpose of arousing the Kundalini. They bring disastrous results when used by ignorant or materially minded people. Sometimes the same issue is achieved when those with mixed motives fling themselves violently into the various religious cults and 'isms'; we hear that their final goal turns out to be a mental home.

Yet another mishap can befall the aspirant who is not sufficiently whole-hearted. If he once arouses the 'serpent', and then subconsciously repents of his endeavours, the serpent rushes downwards and plunges his owner into the worst of orgies and excesses. Unfortunately this sometimes happens to saintly men who have been just a little too ambitious for spiritual gain.

We have to realize that steady, patient, even and balanced progress is the surest way: we must not expect to come to results too easily. Greed of the mental or spiritual body will produce a congestion and sickness on those planes as surely as its counterpart will on the physical. To try and attain mental expansion while still the victim of inhibitions and repressions is like expecting to become a ballet-dancer while still refusing to use certain limbs or muscles. We have so fully to realize the glories of possible attainment that all lesser desires simply fade out—they do not have to be repressed. It is only in the purity of a one-pointed mind (the root-meaning of pure is 'complete') that we can welcome as one of the greatest events of our life the safe awakening of the Kundalini serpent.

The same truth applies in the relation between the sexes, where again sincerity of purpose and wholeheartedness are the determining factors of resulting happiness. When a spiritually minded man and woman fall in love with each other there occurs a blending and a union between the seven-fold bodies of each of them, culminating in spiritual as well as physical creation. This gives an ecstasy and fulfilment seven times greater than that which the average physical union can bring. Force and power are engendered an hundredfold more on all planes through having been conserved instead of frittered away. Both the children and all creative work resulting from such a union would be incomparably superior to the average.

If every child were brought up with understanding and ambition focused upon such an ideal we should soon have a heaven upon earth.

As it is, the subject of sex is so little understood that any irregularities in its manifestation consign the victim to suffering in ignorant and misunderstood wretchedness.

The interplay of the masculine-feminine positive-negative principle throughout our bodies is not yet fully grasped. The ancient wisdom teaches that man, having a positive masculine physical body, has a feminine negative etheric body. This may be why he has in some ways much less staying power in the matter of pain and endurance than woman, who owes her endurance to the fact that in spite of her negative feminine physical body she has a positive or male etheric body.

Man's astral or emotional body is masculine, and therefore active and under his control, whereas woman's astral is negative and absorbing. It is at the mercy of outside influences, and that is why she can be dragged down to lower depths in some ways than a man can. A drunken woman is more terrible than a drunken man.

It would seem to follow, then, that man's mental body has a preponderance of the feminine quality and woman's of the masculine, and perhaps that explains why wise men have always considered that woman can actually take the lead and inspire them from the mental level if she but realizes it and fits herself to do so.

Man is meant to learn sensitivity and intuition from woman, and woman is meant to learn steadiness and honesty from man. A perfect man or a perfect woman must be a complete blending of the qualities of both. That is why we are told that at the end of evolution there will be no differentiation of the sexes. Meanwhile, the processes of this integration bring about temporary aberrations which result, through misunderstanding, in homosexuality and other irregularities.

We are taught that men and women change their sex at various incarnations. This change sometimes produces a masculine woman or a feminine man, until the readjustment is complete.

It is necessary that these things are better understood. Then people, instead of giving way helplessly to any abnormalities which they discover within themselves, and living a life of shame-faced yet defiant indulgence, will learn to master such tendencies and turn them to good account.

When we consider that, from the greatest to the smallest, all progress and evolution depends upon the interplay of the male-positive and female-negative principle, and how this especially applies to the mental and spiritual creative powers to which mankind is dedicated to strive, we begin to see how much futile stagnation is caused either by people who refuse any relationship with the opposite sex, such as nuns and monks, or by those who indulge in homosexuality. The seven bodies of man and woman merge creatively when they work or play together, entirely irrespective of the sexual act, and stimulate and nourish one another in a way which is essential to the bringing through of creative inspiration. In the temples of ancient wisdom, before their degeneration, the priests worked with their female oracles to achieve their greatest results.

When men and women are brought up to be sensitively alive to this interplay of the forces between them, they will obtain so much fulfilment from them that the act of procreation will fall back quite naturally to its normal use. Sex-antagonism and other inhibitions will disappear. There will be produced the perfect working unit, built up of Woman-Wisdom-Strength and Man-Power-Action.

It is upon such units that the Golden Age will be founded.

7

BIRTH, SLEEP AND DEATH

As we have proceeded to explore life along these lines, it has appeared to grow more and more complicated. Indeed, many people will draw back with a feeling of resentment. They will say: 'It is not necessary to know all these things! So far I have managed very well without them. The simple Christian faith is sufficient for me.'

Such people will probably hate the idea of living again on this earth. They are interested neither in the future development of mankind nor in the service which they might contribute to it. In this way they show us that they are possibly still the victims of moral laziness. They are not yet prepared to think deeply or to seek new ways of helping and achieving. They wish to be left in peace in the groove in which they have been brought up.

Nor is it good to endeavour to persuade them otherwise. They are probably doing very well at their present stage, even, possibly, better than those who are so anxious to teach them other ways.

There are plenty who are eager for further knowledge and who need no persuading!

Let us continue our explorations with these latter ones, and consider more deeply the phenomena of man's existence—his birth, his growth, his sleep and finally his death.

It has been said that man is born unfinished! He is born at the ninth month, the 'finished number' being twelve. And certain it is that the young of the human are the most helpless of all.

Throughout this chapter we will study the human being in his fullest sense, that is to say with his seven interpenetrating 'bodies' as before explained.

We are told that the birth of the physical body precedes that of the other 'bodies', each one of which is intimately connected with one of the seven principal Endocrine Glands.

We can do no more than touch on this intricate subject here, in order to give point to our argument. Up to the age of seven the average child has only complete control of its physical body, the rest of its faculties being imitative or dormant. In a court of law a child is not considered punishable until after seven years of age.

After the first cycle of seven years we are told that the 'etheric body' is 'born', or comes under positive control. The ethers govern growth and memory. These are the two functions most prominently active during the next seven years.

At the age of fourteen the astral or 'emotional' body is said to 'come into birth'. This governs the emotions and desires, so this is the age of puberty, and unrestrained emotions. Up to fourteen years the child has been dominated by the Thymus Gland in which was bequeathed a store of red blood corpuscles by the mother. This gland should become recessional by the age of puberty, at which time the child has begun to manufacture its own blood. The blood is known to be the seat of the ego, which can then begin to control the young person, who becomes conscious at this time of his individuality. From now on guidance instead of authority must be the rule.

The Adrenal Glands, which come into dominance at puberty, help to develop the individual driving-force as well as the brain power. They are said to be the 'glands of fight and fright'. Under their government there is extreme sensitivity to fear and anxiety. These tendencies arouse a need for some kind of religious belief to give reassurance. So we find that during these years there is often great emotional piety.

The end of the third cycle of seven years sees the 'birth' of the 'mental body', so that by twenty-one years of age the individual has reached an important epoch in his life. He has accomplished the completion of the three lower 'bodies' of man, the physical, emotional and mental. He has developed into the complete human being (from ordinary standpoints) and is considered to have reached his majority and the state of manhood. From then onwards, if man develops as he could and should do, every further seven years will see the birth of a new quality or power, of a kind more subtle and less easily described here.

Finally, we come to the magic number of seven times seven and man has reached the age of forty-nine. It is here, therefore, that we can expect the flowering of his greatest power and quality. Sure enough we are told that it is at this age that his 'Higher Mind' should come into birth, giving him a subtle capacity for the highest and loftiest achievement. The Pituitary Body and Pineal Gland should now co-operate to use the sum of his life's experience for new creative ideas, deductions and philosophies.

Therefore, at this age, it would indeed be well if man could retire from all mechanical routine work and concentrate on giving to the world his contribution in the way of schemes for the betterment of mankind and the various inspirations resulting from his experience. As he could still have expectation of life for another fifty years, this would allow him close on half a century of potent fulfilment in living. Such would be the programme of the perfected man or woman who was able to live up to his or her potentialities.

But at the present time many people dissipate their energy and strength to such an extent while young that they never reach the flowering of their greatest faculties at all. They live and die without ever tasting the ultimate joys and triumphs of human existence. They are never able to feel that they have made any knowledge really their own—that they *know* any one fundamental fact of life—what they are, why they are here, or to what progressing! They live always like the man who said, 'The only certain thing in life is doubt!' They admit their dark ignorance by scoffing at the bare possibility of such knowledge, refusing to see that right down the ages there has been a vast accumulation of 'circumstantial evidence' compiled for their own heritage and benefit. They continue to muddle along interminably in their stagnant grooves.

Such laziness makes man willing to be blind to the fact that his greatest contribution of value to the world can be expected after he is fifty. Therefore he does not husband his mental and his physical strength to that end. He should realize that the inspired productions of the higher mind give the intense joy of *fulfilment*, than which there is no greater glory.

The fact that many people are half-exhausted wrecks by the age of fifty, and others much before that, is a disgrace to 'progress' and modern education; and one more proof of the prevailing ignorance is that people are not sensible of this disgrace.

When healing the sick Christ said, 'Thy sin is forgiven thee,' pointing out very definitely that disease is the outward manifestation of wrong thinking. But we have not yet taken the hint. We are still proud to tell of our disease, unaware that we are giving away the unclean and unkempt condition of our minds. In the future people will feel ashamed of letting down the community by becoming unwell. A man will be as unwilling to admit to having a cold as he now is to confess to a theft.

The present general ill health is responsible for many irregularities in the development of the glands. Some of them do not recess when they should, and so a childish and unmoral state continues in the growing youth.

Unbalance of the glands causes some of them to predominate too early, to compensate for weakness in others. This produces geniuses, who are, for that reason, often prone to epilepsy and other abnormalities.

The ancients understood the connection between the glands and the subtle worlds of nature. It will be a happy day when that knowledge is revised by modern scientists.

Let us next consider the common but marvellous phenomena of sleep.

There is a vast accumulation of data proving that the ego or individual can and does leave the body during sleep. The blood recedes from the brain, which can then no longer function. Yet much mental activity may take place, together with many authentic experiences of far-away places. A person can, during sleep, solve intricate problems which have beaten him during the day. He can also tell the time and awaken at any hour decided upon. He can function in a complex world of happenings which he calls 'dreams'.

We are told that if the ego leaves the physical body during sleep he does so clothed in his mental and astral 'bodies', in which he is as mobile as electricity. The physical body is left enveloped in its etheric body or double, that counterpart of the human being formed of 'condensed ethers', through which the life-forces are fed to the tissues from the surrounding ethers.

Man's various 'bodies' are linked together by a vital elastic cord, operating rather like an electric current without the wire. This cord is a kind of umbilical cord which joins the ego and his vehicles to that part of Mother Earth which is his physical body. When it snaps he is born into the 'after-life' and we say that he is dead. This cord is referred to in the Bible as the 'Silver Cord'. As long as it is intact the travelling ego is able to get back into his body as surely as a telephone message can travel along the wire.

We are told that the only difference between 'life' and 'death' is the sundering of this subtle link which binds a person to his physical body.

A strong desire to see a friend may often take the sleeper to see that friend, who may be either awake in his physical body or himself travelling, while 'asleep', in the astral realms.

In this way, it is said, many important meetings and actions are rehearsed by the people concerned days before they occur. This would explain why one often has the feeling of knowing just what is going to be said or done. It is possibly in that way that many prophecies are given.

In this connection we should notice the extreme significance which all ancient nations attached to dreams. The power clearly to remember one's dreams was cultivated assiduously by the priesthood, as was also the ability to interpret the dream. An adept in these matters was held in highest esteem by the nation, whose affairs were regulated according to the instructions or prophecies so given. Joseph of the Old Testament was such a case. Cheating or incompetence in these matters was a heinous crime. Josiah of the Bible was told that false dreamers should be put to death. Alexander the Great spoke of dreams as the greatest chance man has of acquiring knowledge.

Martin Luther said that the correct translation of 'He giveth His beloved sleep' is 'He giveth to His beloved during sleep'.

The whole history of the Bible, as well as many other ancient histories, revolves round the importance of visions, prophecies and dreams.

What are we doing now about this interesting activity which takes up nearly a third of our living hours?

The first step would be to obtain through concentration and practice a clearer recollection of our dreams. To do this it is necessary to try to visualize the Astral Plane as it really is. This is difficult because once we are free in the Astral World conditions are utterly different. Then around us pulsates the living malleable astral stuff, which is free from the laws of gravitation, and which moulds itself at once into form under the impetus of our minds. If we want a horse, for example, we involuntarily and rapidly build one with our thoughts, and it is only such a horse as our powers of visualization and observation can produce! So we are told that at night the astral realms are peopled with sleepers surrounded by their 'dreams' or creations, which are sometimes ludicrous in the incompleteness of their conception. Apparently a person can, therefore, either actually meet his friend in sleep or converse with his own conception of his friend, which he has created. How near he gets to his desire depends on the extent of his concentration and will-power.

Another condition of the Astral World is that many things can be happening in the same spot without being aware of one another, as it were, the different grades or vibrations of astral stuff flowing through and interpenetrating without losing their separate identities (in much the same way as we when in physical bodies can walk right through in 'ghost'). Here we enter the realm of the Fourth Dimension. If we have had no personal experience of it, we can only understand it by studying the thousands of descriptions given to us throughout history by those who had.

The jar of returning from those subtler realms into the heavy vibrations of our physical bodies, at the moment of awakening, usually shatters the memory of our experience. We retain at best a jumbled and inconsequent translation of our dream. This is where the need of training comes in. We should concentrate on exercising a strong grip upon ourselves at the instant of awakening. By this simple expedient we may soon learn consciously to profit by our nightly experiences.

Also, before sleeping we should tune our minds to our highest aspirations, as this will determine the realms we are able to reach. If the mind is clogged with petty earthly considerations, such as the price of food or a quarrel with a neighbour, its owner is naturally drawn to the same type of vibration when asleep in the astral world.

Let us now consider what is said to happen when Death has snapped the Silver Cord, and the person is finally separated from his physical body. We are told that often it may take a little while for the individual to realize that he is 'dead'. But for some time prior to this he has been building in the astral stuff the kind of Heaven or after-life to which he aspires.

Of course, thousands build a Heaven with golden streets and angels playing on harps. These numberless living 'thought-forms' cohere by the law of attraction into one great whole, so that the conventional 'Heaven' is actually there awaiting its owners.

Those who expect, because of their guilt, hell-fire and goblins, have created that charming reception for themselves also!

The miser will probably have made for his use a heaven full of nothing but gold pieces. The Eastern pasha will certainly get his Paradise of Houris. The disbeliever in after-life will have created for himself a horrible blank abyss.

We are told, then, that people remain imprisoned in their self-constructed Paradises until they become so weary of the limitations of their own desires that they are gradually freed from them, and the mind is able to expand and aspire to fresh ideals. Eventually the ego is free to pass through these lower astral realms, known as Purgatory, purged finally of petty wishes and conceptions, and enjoy the higher states of Paradise to which it has learnt to orient itself.

We have heard of the Third Heaven and the Seventh Heaven, without probably giving a second thought to those terms. There are apparently vistas of amazing worlds ahead of us which only open up to our understanding in measure as we develop our minds and our aspiration to meet them.

We must realize that life on the Physical Plane is but a fraction of the whole and that the Sage or Yogi of both East and West is endeavouring to train his mind to a state of continued un-broken consciousness throughout waking, sleeping, death, and onwards to the next incarnation upon this earth.

In this way does a man finally become a god.

8

SECRETS OF BREATHING

CONTINUING our study of the phenomena of life we can next consider the universal activity of breathing.

This very strange process is indeed much more widespread than we would at first suppose. We are told that the creation of the world was begun when the Creator 'breathed upon the waters'.

And, again, the symbolical explanation of the creation of man tells how he was formed out of dust, into which was breathed the 'Breath of Life'.

The tremendous importance of Breath could hardly have been more definitely emphasized, but we have paid little attention to the invaluable hints bequeathed to us by those ancient savants in their veiled language. We know that plants breathe, and lately have discovered that metals breathe also. Scientists are busy studying the long-drawn-out rhythms of the sun. If we apply to the mystics on this point they tell us that the sun breathes regularly, each breath taking eleven years, and causing at its fullness the appearance of 'sun-spots' upon its surface. The sun is called the heart of the Solar System. We may suspect that it really *is* the heart of a very vast living Being in Whose breath we have our own breathing and living.

We are familiar with the main chemical aspects of the act of breathing as applied to ourselves.

Primarily, we must contain a definite amount of air, to counteract the law of gravitation which pulls us to the earth. At sea level the pressure is about sixteen pounds to the square inch, and this must be equalized by the intake of air. That is why the lungs never empty all the air they contain. Their total capacity is said to be 250 cubic inches, but they only empty 150, so that there always remains 100 cubic inches of air within them. For this reason, if it is desired to clean and refresh the lungs, very prolonged *outward* breathing is the most efficacious. Nature's way of refreshing us is to cause us to collapse limply into a chair and sigh out a long breath.

In breathing we absorb the Oxygen from the air into our lungs to be used for the production of heat and energy through combustion with the substances contained in our food, and we exhale the (to us) poisons as Carbonic Acid Gas.

The animals breathe in the same way, but plants, on the other hand, need to breathe *in* the Carbonic Acid Gas for their sustenance. Here we have one of the secrets of the give-and-take existing in Nature and the reason why animals and plants could not live without each other.

In a normal human being there are approximately sixteen to eighteen breaths per minute, each taking in thirty cubic inches of air. Each breath consists of inhalation, exhalation, and a pause, the whole process taking up the time of four heart-beats. Our artificial methods of living have gradually ruined the natural quality of our breathing and hardly one person in fifty breathes as Nature intended.

The correct muscular action is as follows:

The lungs are contained within the basket of the ribs, the whole resembling a balloon, which inflates at the intake of breath and deflates at the exhaling. There is a muscle at the base of the lungs which should contract them *upwards* at the inhalation, but in most people the muscle is inactive.

Many breathe downwards into their abdomens, pressing down the already sagging internal organs.

In correct breathing the whole chest is uplifted at the intake of the breath, and this raises up all the internal organs from their stagnant position. At the exhalation the diaphragm muscle aforementioned contracts again *upwards*, dragging up still farther the organs below.

Correct breathing in this manner will of course exercise a continuous gentle massage and stimulation of the digestive organs, thereby ensuring perfect action of the alimentary canal and eliminating the need for pills and drugs. The second important aspect of breathing is the rate at which we breathe, the 'frequency', as we should say in wireless parlance. We have seen that the whole of life is built up by means of different speeds of vibration, and therefore the rate of motion of anything is the most important factor about it, determining what it is. Therefore, we cannot overestimate the significance of the speed and rhythm of our breathing.

'Show me how you breathe and I will tell you what manner of man you are!'

The Yogis and Eastern Sages make a very deep study of breathing and have evolved a profound science from it. By means of this science they profess to accomplish many things, such as prolonging their youth and their years of living, and attaining to various degrees of trance and clairvoyance, by means of which they gain access to knowledge. This science has been handed down from teacher to pupil for thousands of years, and is only accessible to and possible for the very few. But it is said to be a forerunner of the attainment of all humanity in the dim future.

Certain it is that all who wish to obtain any degree of control of their health, characters, or circumstances, must first begin at the very foundation of their lives—their breathing.

Having put in order the mechanical muscular action of breathing, the next thing to consider is the rhythm. We have now to realize that, as not only physical things but also thoughts, feelings and various forces exist all around us *by reason* of their particular *number* or rate of vibration, so we are all the time tuning in to this or that according to our own rate of vibration, which is adjusted by our breathing. We can think of ourselves as wireless receivers, and it is up to our ego or will to tune us in and decide what we shall receive.

I have said that normally there are sixteen to eighteen breaths per minute.

It is said that if the breathing is changed to about twenty-six light breaths per minute it will be impossible after a short time to feel pain!

That is why in the heat of battle terrible wounds can be

received without feeling them at all. It is also why many great feats are accomplished under the stress of excitement. The breath quickens, the blood heats up, and this drives the ego slightly out of the body, so that sensations are little felt. Extreme indulgence in alcohol has the same effect. That is why intoxicated persons seldom hurt themselves. We can do and suffer things in 'hot blood' which we can never achieve in 'cold blood'.

There is an interesting story in the Bible in connection with this.

When Amalek drew the Israelites into battle Moses went to the top of a hill. He held up his arms, using his great hypnotic powers to prevent the enemy from working themselves up to the fighting frenzy in which they would partly leave their bodies. He prevented them from quickening their breathing, and so they had to fight in cold blood and could not prevail. Directly Moses dropped his arms from fatigue the battle would go against the Israelites.

Martial music is designed to quicken the breath and the emotions. So is the colour red on flag and uniform.

It is quite impossible to become excited if one breathes slowly. That is why a person in a rage is asked to 'stop and count ten'; the breathing inevitably slows down and excitement drops.

Some of the sages believe that we have a definite number of breaths allotted to us for our lives. Those who waste them and speed them up in excitability and emotionalism shorten their span. Those who become philosophers in the true sense of the word, balanced, measured and contented, will be able to live to a very ripe old age with unimpaired faculties.

By quickening the breath the body loses its powers of self-protection and exhausts and injures itself without feeling it at the time.

By slowing the breathing down to ten or twelve per minute it will be found impossible to feel excited, irritable or 'nervy'. This is a useful and invisible little exercise with which we can protect ourselves from those states of mind which tend to poison our systems.

If the breathing is reduced to a deep slow rhythm of ten per minute, for five minutes, the brain will become marvellously clear and ready for work. This can be done before taking up any study, the result lasting for some hours.[1] Many of the conflicting vibrations and 'thoughts' which we allow to pass haphazard through body and brain will have been cancelled out by the rhythmic powerful beat brought about by the slower breathing.

If the breathing can be dropped to an even three per minute all the bodily vibratory activities will become so subdued and harmonized that the more delicate psychic perceptions will be discernible, giving us what we call 'inspiration', instinct or pre-monition; for they are the instigators of all great achievement.

The above-mentioned rates of breathing can be used without danger, if practised gradually and intelligently. But it is ex-tremely dangerous for the average person to attempt any of the more complicated systems sometimes unwisely given out, which might lead them into a mental home or worse.

Yogis can slow down the breath to one per minute, which allows them an intensity of concentration resulting in experi-ences beyond our imagination or comprehension. Finally they are able to suspend the breathing altogether and allow themselves to be buried for weeks at a time without coming to any harm.

Breathing must always be performed through the nose, quite silently, steadily, regularly and without strain. It should prefer-ably be practised in a quiet place and not just after eating. While breathing the mind should be focused on the highest ideals and aspirations. Remember that we are breathing in, besides oxygen, nitrogen, and hydrogen, a host of subtle and powerful elements and forces. It is the mind which subconsciously directs the selec-tion and utilization of these powers. We breathe in Life, we breathe in God, according as to what we aspire.

Slow, deep, gentle breathing will cure insomnia, nerves, blood-pressure, fear, brain-fag and bad temper.

The Easterns apparently know many things about breathing with which the Western world is not yet familiar. They believe, for instance, that in correct breathing only one nostril is actually used at a time. This is said to be caused by tissues in each nostril

[1] From a lecture by Robert King.

which swell alternately at intervals, thus allowing full use of only one nostril. There are said to be two currents which pass up and down the spine, the one on the right side being positive and the one on the left side negative (*see* pages 74 - 6).

The breathing, therefore, is performed alternately along an electrical current indrawing 'positive sun-ruled' particles and a magnetic current indrawing 'negative moon-ruled' particles. It is said that by using this knowledge the temperature of the body can be regulated.

Astrologically, a Sign comes up on the Ascendant every two hours, alternately a positive and negative sign, and this is connected with the breathing.

It is said that Indian doctors always study the patient's breathing first of all, being in this way able to determine the condition of the magnetic and electrical areas in the body at the time.

Apparently, after a meal or during the change-over both nostrils are used, so that it takes a little time to determine the exact state of affairs.

An expert in these matters would, however, know the quality of his powers of achievement at any given hour, being thus able to ensure the maximum of creative output with the minimum of expended energy. Whereas all we now know is that we are either 'in the mood' for work or not, and this results in an indifferent and uneven output.

The much-discussed power of levitation, in which a yogi is said to be able to conquer the laws of gravity and rise in the air, appears to have a strong connection with breathing.

A simple little experiment will point this out.

Let one person lie down straight and stiff on a couple of chairs. Let four persons stand round him, one at each shoulder and one at each knee, each one placing a finger beneath their prone comrade. All must then breathe steadily and in unison for a minute or so. Finally, after the intake of breath, raise the prone man into the air upon the tips of the fingers. He will seem to weigh nothing at all.

The Egyptians and earlier races could lift mighty stones by some agency which still puzzles scientists. Were they perhaps able to overcome the laws of gravity by concentrated scientific breathing on a large scale? If four people can lift say twelve stone without feeling it, by breathing in unison, what could a thousand do?

It has been found in some factories that the output of work is much improved by allowing the workers to sing. After all that has been said about breathing it will be realized at once what an enormous power for good singing could be if properly used and understood. There is no end to the benefit to be obtained by combining breathing, rhythm and sound as in singing.

A person who is timid, cowardly or shy narrows his chest and breathes feebly. Diseases such as asthma are probably the direct result of nervous breathing. If we are calm, confident and courageous we breathe deep and slow. As an aid to attaining these qualities we must first correct our breathing.

Everyone should breathe in the divine Breath of Life with all his heart and sing his song of thanksgiving no less regularly than do the birds.

9

SECRETS OF COLOUR

SOME poet has said, 'Colour is not in the rose but in ourselves.'
What *is* colour?

In Chapter 2 we stated that out of the vast scale of Nature's
vibrations a tiny octave is registered by the optic nerves. Our
physical eyes respond to these particular vibrations with a
reaction which we know as colour. If we had no eyes those vibrations would still exist—but as what?

Medical science has proved that different colours have definite
and varied effects upon our nervous systems and that they act
upon us quite independently of our eyes or minds. Their influence
is particularly marked in the case of lunatics.

It has been suggested that Colours are really Rays radiating
down to this earth at their specific rates of vibration. A red rose
reflects back all the colour rays except red, which it absorbs. Our
optic nerves react to its vibrations and we say, 'The Rose is red.'

The perfect blending of the seven colour rays in the bright day-
light gives us a white light. If the rays are split up by being
passed through a glass prism they are at once visible as colours.
In the same way a rainbow is produced by the minute prismatic
effects of rain in the sky. If you walk round a fountain in the sun,
at a certain point you will see a rainbow.

The colour rays are pouring down on the earth night and day.
Every object and every atom responds to them, thereby announc-
ing its own quality to those who are able to decipher the language
of colours.

Where do these rays come from and what are they?

We have noted that the seven major planets of our solar
system are radiating their various forces outwards, so that they
reach this earth at considerable strength. As there are also seven
primary colour rays radiating to the earth we may suspect a

definite connection here, and suggest that colours are really an expression of the planetary rays, observable by us as they are absorbed and held by different objects.

The planets are composed of minerals and chemicals. In each planet one particular metal is said by astrologists to predominate. In Mars it is iron, and in Mercury it is that metal. Just as radium radiates off minute particles of itself for hundreds of years, so do these enormous planets radiate subtle emanations of their own chemical constituents in infinitely fine form. A human being also radiates subtle emanations of everything of which he is composed. A clairvoyant (or person with extra-sensitive sight) is able to see the colours of these rays at a certain angle, and speaks of them as the person's 'aura'.

Let us name the colours in the order in which they appear in the spectrum. We take red first because it has the lowest vibration, being therefore the coarsest and most physically vitalizing; its place on the scale is just above the heat vibrations, and it is heat-giving in itself. As the vibrations increase in speed up the scale we come to orange, then to yellow, then green, blue, indigo and violet, the violet leading us on up into the extraordinarily penetrating and rapid vibrations of the ultra-violet ray.

Let us see if we can connect up any of the information which astronomers, astrologers and scientists give us about colour and the planets. Astrologers tell us that the 'planetary colour' of Mars is red, and that Mars 'rules' or has dynamic power over iron. Now, it is iron which is responsible for our red warm blood —without it we should have some sort of cold pale liquid in our veins. Mars is the home of the god of war, giving a martial spirit to all those born under his Sign, giving quick strength and force, vitality, power and leadership.

If we suppose that the properties of this planet are to be found in its rays which filter downwards and reach this earth as the colour red, then we are not surprised when we find that the effect upon patients of red-coloured electric lamps is to stimulate, warm, excite and cheer; to increase the activity of the arterial blood; to counteract physical inefficiency, paralysis and rheumatism; that red glass windows have much the same effect, and also red walls and decorations to a lesser degree. By the same token red should be avoided by those who contain too much iron, or who are in any condition of heat or inflammation. Red-haired people, excitable lunatics, and bulls should be surrounded by the cooler colours if peace is to prevail!

Proceeding with our investigations we find that red is the chief spectroscopic colour in any herbs or medicines, having a heating and stimulating effect, such as cayenne, cloves, or musk. Finally, we can turn to the discoveries of the famous Dr. Babbitt in chromotheraphy, or healing with colours. He proved that plain water hung up in the sunlight in a sealed chromo-lens of red glass becomes impregnated with certain chemicals in a powerfully healing form, the chief of which is iron! Such water when swallowed has, apparently, the same effect as an iron tonic.

Let us, therefore, when using or thinking of the colour red, bear in mind the following attributes with which scientists or sages have connected it. It is the colour of Mars, whose stone is the ruby and whose metal is iron.

It is the lowest of the seven of the colour scale, and it belongs to the lowest of the seven notes of the musical scale, which is C. When C is played certain sensitive people see the colour red; and most martial music is in the key of C.

Red when predominating in herbs, coloured lights or glass, and surroundings, gives warmth, increased circulation, vitality and energy to the body, and cheerfulness, stimulation and excitement to the spirit. The red flag has been used throughout history for incendiarism. Finally, if dark red is seen in the aura it indicates passion and a fighting spirit!

The second colour in the spectrum is orange. This beautiful colour is associated with the Sun, and has also a warming and invigorating effect. But whereas red is stimulating to the body and the blood, orange is stimulating to the emotions. It cures those states of paralysis which are often due to emotional reaction. It should be avoided by extremely emotional types, who should acquire balance through its complementary colour, blue. Its note is D in the musical scale. Melodies in that key have a strong emotional appeal. The metal belonging to the Sun is gold, from which the alchemists believed they could obtain the Elixir of Life which rendered man immortal. Used as a medicine gold has a very purifying effect.

The third colour in the spectrum is yellow. We are told that this colour belongs to the planet Mercury. Mercury confers a quick intellect by stimulating the nervous system. To be quick-witted the nerves should be in an active condition throughout the body; so nothing can remain stagnant under the beneficial influence of this planet. Wisdom is said to be conferred by Mercury and its colour yellow. Therefore Buddha always clothed his priests in yellow, which colour has stood for wisdom and intellect throughout the ages.

Yellow electric lamps or glass windows stimulate the nerves of the brain and the body and cure a stagnant condition of the internal organs. They should not be used for highly nervous subjects.

We find that yellow predominates spectroscopically in all herbs which are purgatives or nerve-stimulants, such as senna, sulphur, fig juice, tartar, phosphorus and castor oil. An extreme amount of yellow has a disastrously over-stimulating effect upon the nerves, causing death, as with prussic acid and strychnine, which are very yellow. Dr. Babbitt proved that plain water, hung in the sunlight in a sealed lens of yellow glass, becomes impregnated with very nerve-animating properties such as phosphorus and sodium, and that it will have a purgative action if drunk, where possibly other drugs have failed. This lens must not be entirely filled, as it will absorb such highly expansive chemicals from the yellow rays that it would burst if full. It is interesting to learn that the water so treated goes bad in a few days.

Yellow is the third of the colour scale. It corresponds to the musical note of E. Its jewel is the yellow topaz, and it represents *luminosity*. When seen in the human aura yellow, if dark and crude, it tells of deceit, treachery and cowardice (we have all heard of the 'yellow streak'!), but if pale, pure and luminous it shows high wisdom and intellectuality.

Our fourth colour is green, standing in the centre of the scale of seven. It is the meeting-ground between the thermal or heating and expanding colours of red, orange and yellow, and the electrical, contracting, cooling colours of blue, indigo and violet. Green gives stability, endurance and quietude. We are allowed much of it to look at in nature and to partake of as nourishment. Its action is to cool the blood and animate the nerves. It belongs to the planet Saturn, whose metal is lead. Saturn rules the spleen which makes the white corpuscles of the blood. These harmonize the building and destroying going on in the human organism. So people with the luminous green of Saturn in their auras are the harmonizers and pacifiers of the world. They stand for social stability. If the green is dark and crude it tells that its owner, so concerned with the affairs of others, has become 'green with envy'.

Green belongs to the fourth of the musical scale, F, whose melodies, usually in a minor key, sing of the melancholy always associated with Saturn. Its stone is the emerald, which bestows peace of mind. Therefore whether through lights, coloured glass or herbs, green gives an all-round steadying and quietening influence. The green flag and lamp represent safety and speak of the guardianship of those in authority. We are told that on the planet Saturn live our guardian spirits.

Now we leave the heating colours and pass upwards to the cooling, contracting ones—blue, indigo and violet.

These rays have a soothing, narcotic and antiseptic action. They act as sedatives to the vascular and nervous system, subdue mania and angry passions, inflammations, sunstroke, insomnia, eyestrain and all irritated conditions of mind and body.

Sedatives, antiseptics and narcotics contain much of these colours; narcotic flowers are blue and purple; blackberries are valued for their astringent qualities.

Blue belongs to the planet Venus, the giver of love, devotion and harmony. Its stone is the amethyst, the super-sacred of the seven sacred jewels. Pale blue in the aura represents devotion, while dark blue shows fanaticism. One can either be 'true blue' or have a fit of the 'blues', according to one's outlook!

Dr. Babbitt says that blue lenses filled with water and exposed to sunlight become impregnated with chlorine, cobalt, manganese and other properties having soothing and antiseptic action. This water will never putrefy. It acts as a sedative and an antiseptic, and is cooling, especially to the blood.

The musical note of blue is G, a favourite key for the composer of romantic music.

Indigo is the sixth of the colour scale. It is, like green, a meeting-ground for all the colours. Its action through herbs and chemicals is intermediately between blue and violet, soothing both nerves and blood. Its planet is said to be Uranus and its stone is jet. In the aura it shows dignity and high aspirations.

Violet is the seventh and last of the colour octave. It represents the seventh and highest quality which man attains—noble spiritual aspiration. Therefore it has always been connected with the priestly ceremonies. Its musical note is B, in which key much sacred music is written. Its planet is Jupiter, ruling the metal tin and the jewel sapphire. In its medical action it approaches the realm of the violet-ray. It cools the nerves, is magnetic and antiseptic.

Violet-lens water keeps indefinitely, and greatly benefits the hair, eyes and the digestion.

Violet in the aura speaks of honour, spirituality and self-esteem.

Above the violet we begin a new octave of higher and more ethereal colours mostly unseen to the average human eye.

The first is rose, which is the red of Mars transmuted to its higher octave, where it speaks of optimism, hope and spiritualized love. The colours continue in octaves which become more and more sublimated, luminous, pure, and pale until in the end they blend back again into the glorious white light from whence they sprang. When the character of a human being is sublimated and perfected the colours of his aura also resolve themselves into a white spiritual light. In the olden days people were able to see this. They represented it as the halo shining around the head of a saint.

Colours, therefore, are of the very deepest significance to us throughout all phases of our life. They have more influence upon us than we can possibly imagine. If we can use them intelligently, they are the greatest of friends, strengthening, soothing and inspiring.

Dark, drab and dingy colours harm our spirits, morals, and health; they encourage crime, inhibitions, inferiority complexes, suicide and stunted development. They actually prevent the radiation of personal magnetism, the give and take between human beings. They inhibit optimism, inspiration and therefore success.

A glance at some of our streets with their dingy dark bricks and shrieking posters will at once show us one reason why apathy, dullness and poor health are still prevalent.

Brown is the colour of earth and holds us to the earth and to material thoughts. Grey is neutral and useful as a background to other colours. White reflects back all the rays and is therefore cooling and restful. Black absorbs them all and is therefore warm, although neutralized.

The modern trend towards plain, pale pastel shades shows a promising awakening to a new and uplifting colour sense.

A colour campaign intelligently launched would do much to cheer, inspire and invigorate humanity.

10

SECRETS OF SOUND

'In the beginning was the Word.'

Thus is the importance of sound emphasized to us, although so simply and directly that it is easy to miss its significance.

The universe was created by speech—the Creator did not act. He spoke. He said: 'Let there be light,' and there was light.

Let us not pass over these words with a shrug, as if they were charming fairy-tales designed to enthral the naïve peoples of old. The deepest scientific knowledge of all times was always thus veiled by symbolism and by myth, and rich is the reward of every effort at interpretation. Certain of the ancient peoples made a profound study of chemistry. The fact that they chose to give to their chemicals the names of gods and goddesses and to describe their reactions under the guise of myths and 'legends' does not in the least detract from their actual knowledge. On the contrary it may show how much deeper and further they penetrated into the realms of ultimate Causes than men of science do today.

We are told by those teachers of antiquity that the formation of this universe out of chaos was brought about by the Breath and Word of the Creator—by Sound! Certain sounds produced differing sets of vibrations in the ether. Some of these were of such low frequency that they formed particles of what we call 'matter' or physical substance. There could not be Light, as we know it, without minute specks of matter in the ether to reflect it.

We learn that later these particles of matter collided, coalesced, the force of their mutual attraction (or gravity) causing them to commence spinning. The endless arrangements thus formed produced this Solar System and all that is therein. We can gain an idea of the infinite number of these arrangements by considering the vast scale of vibrations with which we dealt in Chapter 2.

The little section of oscillations on this scale, to which the ear can react, and which we know as Sound, are of comparatively low frequency. They occur below the heat vibrations. A vibration of sixteen per second gives the lowest note heard by the human ear, and the scale of sound runs up to nearly 40,000 vibrations per second. This speed is the highest which we can register as sound.

Higher up on the scale, vibrating at about seventy million million million times per second, begin the vibrations which we know as heat, and to which the heat-centres in our skin react. Above these come the Light and Colour vibrations and above those are the X-ray and the subtle vibrations of the mind.

Below the Sound vibrations come those of chemical substances which make up the physical world.

It is said that the whole scale of vibrations is divided up into Octaves of Seven. Each octave is a replica of the others, only functioning at a doubled or trebled speed of vibration. Thus, merely as a simile, supposing the first note of the octave C to vibrate at twenty per second, we might find that a certain number of octaves lower down—the vibrations of the first note of an octave at say perhaps twenty per minute—would be apparent to us as, for instance, the metal iron. The first note of an octave several hundred times higher up on the scale would be apparent to us as the colour Red, and far higher up still, as the emotion of anger or passion. All these different expressions of one note or vibration, as well as many others in between, are ruled, controlled, or emanated from the planet Mars according to certain schools of thought, and express the good and bad qualities which are associated with that planet.

By studying such theories we can realize the intimate connection between Sound and all other expressions of life. Sound is low down on the scale and comes just above Form. *Therefore Sound is the intermediary between the 'abstract' idea and the 'concrete' form.* Sounds mould the ether into shapes, and through these shapes the corresponding Power is able to play and make its impress on physical matter.

The clairvoyant primitive peoples actually saw the shapes produced in the ether by sounds. They represented these shapes as the letters of their alphabet. So most words and sounds of the early languages actually controlled and represented that which they expressed. When those people called on the god 'Ra' they established a connection just as definitely as we do when we tune in our wireless to Paris or London.

Throughout history we can learn of the deliberate and effective use of sound. Priests have always employed it, creating certain definite reactions on the people by the use of chanting and intoning. In the Ancient Mysteries and Magical Ceremonial Rites words, sounds and shapes were combined to gain certain ends. Each one of us is intensely affected by sound-waves, which of course pass right through our bodies.

Every object and every person has a key-note—in other words the sum of their vibrations responds to one particular note or chord of the musical scale. If a person's note or chord is sounded gently and melodiously it has a healing and constructive influence upon him. If it is sounded loudly, harshly and continuously it has a correspondingly destructive influence, making that person ill and unhappy. If you can discover the note belonging to a particular wine-glass and sound it loudly into the glass for a little while you will shatter the glass to pieces. It is said that the walls of Jericho fell because of this same law, as the key-note of the wall was purposely sounded with continuous harshness by the trumpets, under the instructions of someone with a knowledge not uncommon in those days.

An instrument has lately been invented called the eidophone. It contains a tightly stretched drum surface upon which a paste is spread. Sounds and words are then uttered underneath this drum. They cause beautiful shapes to form in the paste, exact replicas of trees, ferns and flowers as they are in nature.

If sand is spread on the drum instead of paste the sounds will produce geometrical designs instead of plant forms. It is even said that ugly and obscene words will produce ugly and displeasing patterns, and the reverse! This experiment proves the creative aspect of sound and helps us to visualize the definite forms and radiations set up in the ether by our own words.

The sounds with which we are surrounded in present-day city life are mostly harsh, monotonous and unbeautiful. If the roar of the traffic were suddenly to cease as we walked down the street we should find that we had been screaming discordantly at our companion to make ourselves heard. Our pleasures also are mostly crudely noisy. At the average cocktail-party everyone shouts at once. The hostess is disappointed if it is not so, while some of the dance music is harsh beyond words. Tube, train and bus all add their quota to the barrage of hideous noise which we have to endure. People who are obliged to listen day after day to sounds which are a discordant offence to Nature's laws will inevitably become sick or depleted, and soon be suffering from one of those innumerable nerve complaints which are the order of the day.

The only way to counteract these bad effects would be by healing the damaged nerve centres with soothing harmonies or with the blessed balm of complete silence for a short period every day. If a person is able to discover his own key-note or chord and to play it over gently to himself he will revive as if by magic. One's key-note can be ascertained by listening to some good orchestral music. When the note is played it will send a thrill right through its owner.

If a person's life is in some way inharmonious or destructive this can be detected at once in his voice, which will often jar upon the listener's nerves; whereas one who is living in accordance with divine law will have a melodious, pleasing voice. The more advanced types of people have resonant voices, while primitive types have the flat 'chest' voices such as are heard among natives, gypsies or the apaches of Paris.

The creative use of sound can be observed on all sides. The baby cries to promote its own growth. Until the little one has uttered its first cry its progress is not assured.

It is said that the birds set up the vibrations which promote the growth of the young leaves by their singing in the early spring. When the leaves are all full out the birds' songs cease, except at twilight and at dawn, at which times the chemical activities of the plant life change. At night plant life breathes out carbon dioxide, although during the day it breathes out oxygen. The times of the change-over are heralded by the birds.

The ancient Japanese mystics such as the Zen monks were said to be able to bring the dead or dying back to life by uttering a certain loud cry. An interesting description of this can be found in the novel *The Garden of Vision*.

Some people assert that in order to connect ourselves with power and wisdom we should go apart to a quiet place and call our own Christian name over and over very gently. Uttering a noun or name creates a form in the ether which acts as a 'receiving station' to certain powers which then play through it. Tennyson declared that he could leave his own body consciously, and gain much experience, by calling his own name. He describes this in the 'Ancient Sage'.

The potent action of sound has always been recognized and applied throughout history; but at the present time a stringent tackling of the Sound problem is urgently needed.

An anti-noise campaign is actually in existence, but its efforts are not much in evidence as yet, and have not received the whole-hearted public support which they deserve.

The medical profession is experimenting with the healing properties of sound. But it is up to every individual to take a personal interest in this vital problem and all the infinite possibilities connected with it.

Those who really wish to get the best out of life should shun inharmonious noises and all superfluous chatter; they should feed their spirit and nerves with music; they should sing often, aiming more at rhythm and resonance than at loudness and high notes; they should study the tones of their own speaking voices to gain an insight into their own characters. They should watch and guard their own words, remembering that in speaking they are building definite forms for good or for evil, which will persist in the ether, connecting their owner permanently with good or evil influences, and attracting to him much that he may ignorantly consider he has not deserved.

Lastly, they should remember that, as all the sages and wise ones are aware, the greatest inspiration and wisdom has been bestowed upon humanity during periods of profound and complete silence.

11

THE SCIENCE OF NUMBERS

THE world is built up of thousands of differing rates of vibrations, all these having their origin in the One original vibration of the mind of the Creator—or the sum, essence or single number of the Whole.

We learn from the ancient teachings that the One original mighty Creative Power, wishing to make further manifestation, and to exercise His creative ability for a purpose which it is beyond us to understand at present, divided Himself (by the power of the Word) into Three, thus forming that great Triangle which originated Life and Action as we know it.

The Triangle, known as Father-Mother-Son, or Positive-Negative-Combustion, or Mercury-Sulphur-Salt, as we have seen, has always been studied all over the world.

We begin, therefore, in this science, with the number One, the Creator, who divides into Three in the act of creating. The scientist will describe this formation as Polarity. As Schopenhauer put it: 'Polarity, or the sundering of a force into two quantitively different and opposed activities, striving after reunion . . . is a fundamental type of almost all the phenomena of Nature, from the magnet and the crystal to man himself.' The Hindus describe it thus: 'Brahma, that the world might be born, fell asunder into man and woman, became name and form, time and space.'

In a further definition of the origin of this Solar System we are told that the Creator, a Great White Light, divided into Three— Red, Yellow and Blue (the primary colours which correspond with the primary notes of the scale, C, E and G). After the division into Three, the second great division into Seven took place, and the Seven Spirits Before the Throne, inhabiting the Seven Sacred Planets of this Solar System, came into being.

From them radiated the seven colours of the spectrum. There are also the seven notes of music, the seven planes of matter, seven days of the week, the seven ages of man and his seven glands—in fact, as we have seen, the tremendous scale of Nature's vibrations runs in an infinity of octaves of seven.

In history we can trace man's appreciation of the significance of the number Seven when we think of the 'Seven days of Creation', Seven Cardinal Virtues, Seven Deadly Sins, Seven Wonders of the World, Seven Towers of Constantinople, Seven Hills of Rome, Seven Plagues of Egypt, the Seven-branched Candlestick—and even the Seven-league Boots!

Seven, therefore, is the number of the condition of man's physical existence upon the earth as it is at present. But humanity is imperfect, unfinished, unevolved, so seven is not the final number. Mankind, as well as all of Nature, is to rise out of the imperfect state, to become complete and creative, and to develop the full quota of qualities and capacities, which run up to the finished number of twelve.

To this end man has to evolve under the discipline of the Twelve Signs of the Zodiac as described in Chapter 5.

These signs circle round the Sun and represent the twelve great lessons and qualities of living. We therefore find this number Twelve playing a significant part in Nature also, as well as in mythology and history. We can at once call to mind such divisions as the twelve hours of the day and the twelve months of the year.

There were also the twelve sons of Jacob, symbolizing the climax of a past period, and the Twelve Apostles, representing the climax of the present era.

When humanity has taken its degree in the school of earthly life, and graduated through all the twelve great tests, becoming thereby master of itself and all conditions, and therefore creative, it turns 'back to the Father' as in the tale of the prodigal son. It has exhausted the possibilities of matter, has realized the illusion of the infinite divisions of nature, and retraces its steps back to the one original great White Light of Omniscience. Man has become One in understanding with the Creator.

The farther we go back in history the more profound seems the understanding of these definitions of life. The ancients arrived at a deep knowledge of astronomy, astrology and world history without apparently possessing any of our instruments of science. We are told that they obtained this knowledge through the subtler senses, by meditation. They discovered many things about the formation, quality and meaning of the universe which could not be expressed in words but only in numbers and symbols, and many of the vital truths of life are still only to be found in this way. Numbers and symbols play a very large part in all the Bibles and sacred writings of the ancients. We should gain much by being able to decipher them.

Everyone who was allowed to study the Mysteries with the learned priesthood of Egypt and Chaldea was initiated into the meanings of numbers and symbols. It is said that first Moses and then Jesus studied in this way. Pythagoras studied thus with the priests for twenty-five years in Memphis, Thebes and Babylon and, as a result, founded his famous school of philosophy. He called his pupils 'mathematicians'. He said 'God geomatrises'. He studied the numerical relationships of all the phenomena of the universe and was able finally to classify and sum them up.

Numbers rule nature, not only in the classification of objects but in periods of time. The Moon plays a large part in this, moving in periods of four weeks, or four *sevens*, ruling woman also in these cycles, and governing the tides and seasons, fertility and growth.

The Moon passes through one of the Zodiacal Signs every two hours. The earth herself, moving on a grander scale, passes through one of the Great Zodiacal Signs about every 2500 years. Certain influences are therefore radiated down to earth by the Moon in miniature changing every two hours, and by the Sun in magnitude changing about every 2500 years. The scientist or astrologer who can decipher the lesser influence can be sure of the greater one. It was in this way that the ancient peoples were able to 'prophesy' the trend of civilizations and races 2000 or 200,000 years ahead. Much of this knowledge is wrapped up in the mistranslated symbolism of the Revelations.

It is therefore apparent that one way of learning many of the secret processes at work in the universe and in our own natures lies in the understanding of numbers and symbols. To do this we must study the output of those early peoples and understand the foundation and origin of their knowledge, and the way in which they were able to tap the 'Universal Mind'.

If a doctor, knowing the periods of crisis and the duration of a certain disease, were to tell a company of the microbes just what would happen to them in three days' time, that would seem an impossible and wonderful feat of prophecy to the microbes; and as they only live from a few minutes to a few hours the prophecy would apply to their far-distant descendants in the dim future. If, however, the microbes themselves could train their mentalities (and science has now proved that even a cell or a microbe has a mentality) they could obtain telepathic contact with the mind of the doctor, and themselves discover his ideas and knowledge of their future development.

Mankind may be said to bear an analogous position to the microbes. We are little more than microbes upon the body of a great Being, which body we call the earth. Just as we depend for our future health, comfort, peace and the development even of our wisdom upon the well-being and co-operation of the cells in our body, so, we may imagine, does that Being depend upon us for His own progress, and in helping ourselves we help Him! If we make progress He is possibly just as grateful to us as we are to our own hands, eyes or brain as they improve in their capacity to serve us well.

Having visualized man as a microbe upon the living body of the earth, let us go further. The Sun is called the Heart of the Universe—why? Because, we are told, it *is* a great heart, the heart of a Being too vast for us to conceive of, and in whose structure our earth plays the part of a gland or organ.

This Gigantic Being is He whom some of us call God, just as we ourselves are a vast inscrutable all-knowing God to the little creatures whom we know as the cells of our own bodies.

In all reverence we might try also to realize that the glorious

Being whose heart is the Sun may also be worshipping and striving to reach a still mightier God even further from our power to comprehend. So life repeats, up and down the scale of size, forward and backwards upon the scale of time, periods and cycles. It is only by having the clue to the octaves and their numbers that we are able to link up and connect and interpret the manifold different expressions of the few fundamental qualities of evolving creation.

These hidden truths constitute some of the Mysteries which the Initiates and Adepts are able to reach, one by one, as they graduate upwards through the school of life, taking one Initiation after another. In olden days certain people were carefully selected to be trained to this end in the temples, although now the road is open to all.

Those early scholars realized that certain sounds linked them up with certain creative principles in nature and that every sound and quality had its *number* which was the sum total of its vibrations.

The science of numbers, or numerology, has, like much of the ancient knowledge, become through disuse misunderstood and debased to the rank of superstitition. It is only used now from the limited personal viewpoint, but even so it can be both interesting and helpful.

It is said that before birth we are drawn to our names, birthdates and parents by an irresistible affinity with those vibrations which compose our own characters and aspirations, and that a numerologist by studying the former is able to tell us what we are and wherein lie our potentiality, our hopes and our hazards. Each letter and date represents a number. The right reading of these numbers will describe our character and type of life. Each number represents a planet, colour, quality and experience in either its good, bad, or negative aspect. We can map out the life according to the relation in which all its numbers are standing to each other.

Those who believe in this science declare that it is extremely useful in the choosing of vocations and partnerships and that with its help the handicap of incompatibility can be avoided.

Like everything else it must be used with moderation and common sense and not in a spirit of idle superstitition.

The famous American physician Dr. Abrams invented an apparatus which measures the vibrations of all the reactions of the human body. He ascertained that every disease has its own numerical value, and that the cure can also be determined by means of numbers. Much, of course, has to be learned and proved about this science, but here again the fundamental importance of a number is brought to light.

The meanings of the primary numbers have been described throughout the ages as follows:

The number One represents the first necessary qualities of evolving life, the pioneer fighting spirit, leadership and force. A person born on the first of any month will be given chances to exercise these qualities.

The number Two represents the second stage in man's developing nature—*sociability*, and includes affection and all the give-and-take qualities, such as diplomacy and home-making.

The number Three represents self-expression. Man has fought and made friends. Now he wants to give entertainment, beauty and *joie de vivre*. People with this birthdate should not be expected to be very orderly or reliable.

The number Four stands for the solid framework of life, the foundations. People attuned to this number will be called the 'backbone of the country'. They are the patient, reliable plodders.

The number Five represents the Five Senses—Experience. It gives travel, variety and drama to life, and *progress*.

The number Six represents Family Life, but on a much broader scale than the retiring number Two. Six stands for Guardianship, when a man begins to sense his higher destiny and responsibilities, to care for all families as well as his own, and to offer world-wide hospitality and help.

The number Seven represents the final turning of man inwards to the spiritual life, to the study of sciences and truths, discipline and organization. It is the number of loneliness.

In number Eight, man, having found his own soul and the power within him, must turn to earth-life once more and learn to combine the two. So eight gives power, organization, and constructive leadership, backed by spiritual inspiration.

The number Nine represents the perfect and completed man, who having fully developed himself, must now forget himself in Sacrifice and Service. Here we have the great lover, humanitarian and artist. Through this number beats the most high-powered of human vibrations, which has great force to be used for either good or evil.

To write all that is known about numbers would fill volumes. We have not space to do more than take this glance at the primary numbers. They, of course, each belong to their Colour, Planet and Sound. When, after some study, it is seen how completely all these facets of life dove-tail and fit into their places like an intricate vast Chinese puzzle it will be realized that these marvellous 'theories' are too perfect and too near to the truth to have been invented by the brains of human beings. This indeed is the reward of a study of these matters—a gradual realization of the amazing fact that there really *is* a whole universe of marvels and of sublime promise for those who seek.

The science of numbers is exhaustive, instructive, and useful if applied with an honest desire for progress and understanding. Modern scientists are busily expressing the ancient beliefs in their own manner. They are measuring the vibrations of diseases, of thoughts, of will-power and of many other activities and getting them all *numbered*. They are numerologists in their own way, although they still turn their backs rigidly upon the ancient sciences. Nevertheless, they are bringing to light one fundamental fact, and that is that everything exists through the formation of a different number, and therefore that numbers *must* constitute a language, a key, and a clue to many secrets in life, if we can learn to decipher them.

There are various systems of numerology. The sifting of the true from the false will do much to develop the student's own powers of deciphering numbers.

12

DIET AND EXERCISE

PEOPLE all over the world are becoming more and more health-conscious.

Very much is being thought, written and tried out in the realms of Diet and Exercise.

At one end of the scale we have those who continue deliberately to 'dig their graves with their teeth', living grossly, carelessly and unnaturally, and indeed 'selling their birthright for a mess of pottage'.

At the other end of the scale we find the 'cranks', people who may end in an asylum or a nursing-home through overdoing things and lacking moderation in their search for the perfect state.

In the middle of the scale we find the people who are as much put off by the cranks as they are by the slovens, and continue in doubt as to how seriously they should treat the whole subject.

It will be well, therefore, to take a comprehensive glance at the question of physical fitness and decide what are the few essentials necessary for its maintenance. It is of paramount importance to realize that the body is built by the mind or ego. We *are* what we *think*. It is the ego which drives the machinery, which directs the habits of the brain, and which selects from the elements of food and air just what it chooses to use. That is why one person will keep healthy and happy on a few grains of rice while another will perish of 'undernourishment' on a quite fair diet. No amount of food, air or exercise will help anyone unless he has the will to be well and the will to be happy, and if he has these qualifications then he will be comparatively independent of his air, food or exercise! This is the first fundamental truth to realize about health. We are as healthy and as happy as we wish to be. If we know how to live, how continually to adore and accept the Divine Will in whatever guise it is working out, and never to act contrary to the tide of Nature, then health and joy will abundantly flow through us, irrespective of accidental man-made conditions.

Most people have not a living faith. Even a quite sincere Christian goes about in a perpetual state of worry, about himself, others and the world in general.

We can only progress through painful experiences, therefore we should welcome such events with keenness!

If we believe that death is a gate to a brighter life then we should never fear it.

We are not logical, and we only half believe things. Therefore our minds are divided against themselves, and this constitutes an inner conflict which naturally poisons and undermines our systems.

The first essential to health, therefore, is to believe—to believe in ourselves, our power over ourselves and our destinies.

The second thing to recognize is that we are meant to be happy. We have not been given the wealth of beauty and wonder which surrounds us on all sides merely to ignore it. We have not been given bodies capable of a hundred enjoyments merely to deny them. For centuries thwarted and jealous kill-joys have been busy misinterpreting religion and human nature, insulting and slighting the very works of their Creator in the natural human functions. If only they had taught Love and Love and again Love in its fullest sense, people's hearts would have become too full and too broad to need to resort to petty physical indulgencies for the capturing of a faint reflection of the Universal Union!

The body should not be disdained, misunderstood or driven to death. It is our wonderful servant, our intricate tool, and the sacred temple of our inspirations. Therefore we must cherish it and nourish it, remembering that joy is the greatest of all nourishment.

We must learn how to enjoy, and that this faculty lies within us, *not* without us. A blind man chained in a dungeon has yet the capacity for infinite joy within himself. And we who are free can drink in joy from a little square of blue sky, a twinkling star, a budding leaf, or a flake of snow; we can find a world of wonder in the eye of a fly or the instinct of a building swallow.

We must also enjoy the many delicious things which constitute man's food. We must make of eating a sacrament, not a grossness, nor a dull necessity. When we eat we are performing a miracle, but the miracle is only as complete as the enthusiasm which we apply to it.

From a physical point of view we are the result of what we eat and how we eat, so we must never forget to treat our period at the table as an event entirely unto itself. Those people who gobble hurried, over-large or meagre meals while screaming with laughter or frantic with worry, and with their minds in a state of rush or restlessness, are committing sacrilege and suicide in subtle form.

It is not of much use to concern ourselves with diet until these primary matters are attended to. We can easily sum up the first essentials as follows:

Deep, slow breathing produces a supply of oxygen for the combustion of food. One should never eat while breathless, hurried, worried, or upset. Calm down first, remembering that nourishment taken by a person in such condition turns to poison —in fact, it is much better to miss a meal altogether, waiting until the system has recovered.

Many people do not realize what a large part of the digestive process should take place before the meal is swallowed. That is why the importance of slow and thorough mastication is always emphasized. A very necessary part of the nourishment can best be absorbed through the walls of the mouth. People who bolt their food have to exist without this primary stage of the digestion. While in the mouth most of the vital *living* forces of the food are meant to be abstracted; but, once swallowed, the acid digestive juices neutralize these forces and part of the potency of the food is lost. Quick eaters do not obtain the stimulation to the brain and nerve-forces which is the reward of eating slowly.

It is a mistake to drink with meals. Food should be taken as dry as possible, without being drowned in liquid or sauces, as this prevents the digestive juices from contacting the food. Drinking should take place before eating or in between meals. Animals do not drink and eat at the same time. Remember always to eat too little in preference to too much. This will be easy once the speed is reduced!

Many people eat an appallingly complicated mixture of foods at one meal, most of which are incompatible. Adults should be very sparing with starchy foods, which are no longer so necessary to them. They should not take starch with acid-making foods such as meat, as this causes fermentation. The famous British lunch of roast beef is ruined by its accompaniment of bread, Yorkshire pudding, potatoes, peas and pastry tart, which array of starch turns the meal into an outrage! Instead of starch we should concentrate upon those foods which give us mental and nervous energy, containing phosphorus and 'vitamins', such as green vegetables, fruits and salads. We should remember that everything which we are able to eat in its raw state is more than twice as strengthening as cooked food.

Another primary necessity for health is the complete *natural* elimination of all waste matter from the body. Lack of this achievement is the fundamental cause of almost all disease. It can be assured by correct breathing (*see* Chapter 8), sparing diet containing roughage, an intensive chewing of all food, and naturally induced perspiration.

If these few simple rules are followed and whatever changes to be effected in the diet are made gradually, a sure foundation for physical fitness will be built up, without the individual becoming a crank or a pest to himself or others. But the most important of all is thorough mastication.

A twenty-four hours' fast taken every three or four weeks will be of extreme benefit, and can do no possible harm, as long as the faster does not wish to think that it is killing him! If he is really too terrified of the extreme danger of this proceeding, he might bring himself to miss one meal occasionally. These little attentions give a chance to the internal organs to perform a much-needed 'spring-clean', which they are always anxious and willing to do if given the chance.

A great many people are perturbed by the question as to whether or not to eat meat. An authority stated in the newspaper recently that the consumption of meat is falling rapidly, and that the choice seems to be whether to return to meat-eating and the strong warlike nature of our forefathers or to give it up and become more peaceable and gentle. As the whole world is crying out for peace and brotherliness, the latter course would certainly seem to be the more desirable.

No idealist or advanced person really likes the idea of eating meat. Many believe that it is a barbarism which will gradually disappear with the passing of the 'Dark Age'. It is quite possible to be strong and active, as many are, on a meatless diet, but after half a lifetime of meat-eating many systems may find a temporary difficulty in readjustment. Here again 'crankiness' must be avoided. Meat may gradually be relinquished until there is a sound knowledge of the necessary substitutes, such as nuts and cheese. But apart from any question of principle, most people would improve in health in measure as they gave up all flesh foods.

The question of alcohol and smoking naturally arises at this point. There again it must be an individual concern for each person. Alcohol is an artificial stimulant and a poison. Its action if taken in any quantity is to drive the ego partly out of the body. The ego can only use the body when it is of a certain temperature. Extreme cold forces the ego out, and unconsciousness ensues. Overheating has the same effect, resulting in fainting or the delirium of fever.

Constant driving out of the ego through alcoholism loosens its grip upon the body and allows outside entities or influences to gain admittance, with the various and dire results, such as obsessions and deliriums while the victim is still partly conscious of the lower astral world (alas, those snakes and rats are not 'imagination'!).

No self-respecting and earnest person will care to indulge unduly in any stimulant, drug, sedative (such as smoking), excitement or emotionalism which prevents him from being entirely himself and the captain of his own soul.

Nevertheless, a sudden violent reactionary effort towards complete abstention in any of these matters may have, of course, an equally over-balancing effect upon the individual. Common sense, moderation, and a love of the natural joys of living will keep the situation under control. For instance, discrimination between raw spirits and delicate wines is a case in point.

Hand in hand with the question of diet comes the problem of exercise.

It is recognized, now that men and women have no longer strenuously to hunt for and prepare their food, that they need a substitute for the exercise they would obtain if living in a 'natural' state. In other words, human beings have a tendency, unless otherwise obliged, to sink into habits necessitating only those few movements which the routine of their lives demands. They mostly move of necessity and not from pleasure. True, we are learning to 'take exercise', but the same exercises, such as tennis or cycling, are liable to be taken by any and everyone, irrespective of their particular nervous or muscular condition. There have been many cases of an overstrained business-man dropping dead at his game of golf for the simple reason that additional concentration was the last thing he needed. College rowing also sometimes results in an overstrained heart which may handicap the unfortunate youth for the rest of his life.

It is a magnificent thing that physical culture is claiming public attention and enthusiasm, but it is not quite such a simple whole-sale affair as may be imagined. A little individual knowledge and intelligence applied to it will do much to aid the authorities. In the pressure of modern life many of us get quite a lot of move-ment. We rush from one place to another, anxious and hurried, with our muscles tensed up rigidly most of the time. In this case our exercises should be *relaxing* ones, designed to counteract the tension of our lives and give our nerves and muscles a rest. Most people are quite unable entirely to relax their brain, nerves and muscles. If they could once learn to do so for a short time each day they would rapidly grow young again!

The second thing to consider is our habitual position, according to what our work is. Those people who spend many hours bent double over a desk are not helping themselves by bending again over a golf-club. They must choose a form of exercise which bends the spine in the opposite direction. It will be seen that serving at tennis has somewhat this effect, although actual back-stretching exercises are better. Swimming is a fine exercise for the spine.

If we turn to Nature, we can see at once the exercises which animals take. Cats and dogs stretch themselves, shake themselves and roll upon the ground. We cannot do better than learn from Nature. After sleeping or working we should stretch and stretch, and stretch again, in every direction we can think of, both lying down and standing upon our toes. Particular attention should be paid to relaxing the back of the neck, as that is the portion of the spine which is kept most continually and unnaturally tensed. It is tensed in thinking. Sleep is only possible when *complete* relaxation at the back and base of the skull takes place.

After having stretched until every single ligament in our bodies has had its turn, then let us shake ourselves. Stand up in bare feet and relax every muscle loosely. Then shake yourself about, imagining that you are both intoxicated and boneless! Continue this until you are sure that every single muscle has relaxed. Then lie down and try to relax the whole of the legs and feet. Follow this with deep, slow breathing.

These exercises may sound strange to those who are accustomed to Swedish drill. Drilling has also its advantages for strengthening and using the muscles, but relaxation correctly performed achieves a release and refreshment for the nervous system not to be found in any other way.

The Western idea of exercise seems mostly to consist of violently agitating every limb of the body in turn, until reduced to a state of exhaustion.

The Easterns exercise in such a way as to conserve instead of expend energy. It is said that those who join the sacred schools of physical culture and are trained by the Yogis learn to exercise while sitting still in one posture and concentrating upon each nerve and muscle. They use special postures to stimulate any given nerve in the body or brain. It is said that in this way they can cure any disease, acquire a fine physique and live a phenomenally long life. The modern osteopath is beginning to discover possibilities of this nature also, but, of course, he works from the outside.

Rolling on hard ground is an excellent form of massage which tones up the muscles and disperses soft fat.

The finest exercises, then, are those in which the animals indulge. Next in order comes the equally natural exercise of swimming.

Other more violent forms of sport may not always be beneficial. In any case, their drawback is that directly they are discontinued the muscles suffer from the changed conditions and the victim may grow plumper than ever, or develop rheumatism. It is often remarked how champion athletes are liable suddenly to succumb to diseases which do not defeat the weedy little man!

The question of exercise must therefore be approached individually and not collectively, bearing in mind that our chief object should be to counteract the tensions and postures of our daily life, and to cultivate a simple joy in the suppleness of our bodies and the ecstasy of free and rhythmic movements.

PART TWO

13

THE 'THIRD EYE'

IN THE preceding chapters a bird's-eye view has been taken of the conditions surrounding developing humanity.

The possible fruits of a deeper understanding of various aspects of life have been considered, such aspects, for instance, as the planetary influences by whose aid we develop, and which we can study through astrology and numbers, and by their manifestations through Colour, Sound and Form. A little research has brought to light the possibility that the discoveries of men of science today may coincide with the knowledge of the mystics of all times, with a difference only of presentation and nomenclature, and the fact that the Mystics always postulated an ultimate Cause and Law behind all phenomena, while present-day scientists seem afraid to link up with such big issues.

Finally we have considered the perfecting of our physical life through more intelligent control of diet, exercise and the human relationships.

Let us now draw away the Veil still further and take a peep at what may be the future awaiting man when he struggles out of the rut of materialism and finally takes the reins of his life into his own hands. It looks as if the Powers that Be are tantalizing humanity into making this effort, because they are allowing hints and bits of knowledge to filter through in a more *general* way than ever before. We find all sorts of unexpected people playing enthusiastically with these jewels as if they were bright new toys. On every hand we hear glib talk of trances, visions, healings and divine guidance. We hear of intimate relationships with the 'Masters', of mystic experiences upon the 'Path'. We are given full details of 'Initiations', reincarnations, and Magic Black and White! Hundreds of societies and cults with scores of 'Teachers' have sprung up everywhere like a mushroom growth—and of course they mostly claim to be the especial instrument of the 'Great White Lodge'.

Now, it may be that many of these people are childish, and that some of them remain materialistic, and jealous, and even profiteer with their spiritual goods!

Nevertheless, two things stand out.

Firstly, there is a growing widespread demand for enlightenment on these subjects, and a deepening sense of the existence of such knowledge. Secondly, everything that is being given out everywhere bears the same stamp, posits the same laws, and makes fundamentally the same promises, in spite of superficial and surface differences. It would all appear to come from one original source, and that source to have been the very ancient teachings of the greatest Sages and Mystics of all times, which has existed the world over in much the same form.

And although people are still perhaps infantile and naïve over the treasures of knowledge so freshly re-presented to them, yet their interest is intense and their numbers are growing.

Furthermore, as in all their various forms these teachings yet tally in laying emphasis on brotherhood, unselfishness, generosity and Peace, they would seem to form some kind of opposition to the propensities for slaughter, oppression, greed and selfishness which are causing widespread havoc in various parts of the world.

True, among these cults are to be found many cranks, hypocrites and other undesirables; but these people would exist in any case. They may have more chance of regeneration where they are. It is necessary always to distinguish between the Teaching and the Teacher; it is possible to learn beautiful truths from a very unbeautiful character, who in that way may be working off his 'Karmic' debts.

The great revival of interest in 'occult' subjects began towards the close of last century. It is said that the close of any century ushers in a foretaste of the knowledge to be assimilated in the next. Certain it is that fifty* years ago there was an intense pioneering activity in research, both 'occult' and 'scientific'. The Theosophists, Christian Scientists, and Spiritualists, the Hypnotists, the Mesmerists and Healers resulted from these activities, to

* Written in 1937!

which were drawn many eminent men and women of the time, who have left behind a wealth of printed records of their studies and testified experiments. Much of all of these results may be doubted by the sceptics—but there is no smoke without fire. The impartial enquirer will do well to observe that in all these diverse activities much the same type of manifestations, information and mysterious laws appears to have come to light.

Those who were studying these things from the mental and philosophical angle were headed by a remarkable woman called H. P. Blavatsky, whose strange personality seemed rather divorced from her profound and level-headed writings. She made a deep and exhaustive search into ancient Eastern mystical records and produced almost an encyclopedia upon the subject in her *Secret Doctrine* and other books. The Theosophists, headed by Annie Besant, carried on the work. During the same period a very ancient sect called the Rosicrucians were allowed to begin to give out a little of their knowledge to the public. Some of this work was accomplished by Rudolph Steiner and men like Max Heindel. The less intellectually inclined were provided for by the Spiritualists, Christian Scientists, Mesmer, Dr. Coué, and others.

Everything was done by fair means, and possibly foul, to awaken people to a sense of the potency of the inner worlds. The seeds thus sown germinated and persisted. Today there is a big field of these activities, which excites little comment because it has grown to be a part of the life of the public.

What are the principal elements of the more exalted of these teachings?

We hear first of all of the great *Plan* for the evolution of humanity, which develops through Spirit ensouling seven great Races and dwelling on seven great Continents, of which Lemuria and then Atlantis were the first two. The earth itself is to have seven successive incarnations before becoming spiritualized. All this is only a tiny little cog in the wheel of Planetary Evolution. Planets come into successive births just as does humanity, both individually and collectively, and so do Solar Systems!

Presiding over our Solar System is the Hierarchy, and all their

staff of graded helpers, mentioned in the Bible as the Seven
Spirits before the Throne, the Archangels, Angels, Cherubim
and Seraphim. Humanity is in the School of Earth, graduating to
be qualified to fill such exalted positions in the dim future. The
first to pass these mystic examinations (called Initiations) will be
ready to replace those of the celestial company who are pro-
moted to higher positions. Having attained such status They
have no longer any need of earth-lessons, but They sometimes
elect to come back to help humanity and set them an example of
the perfect human life, as did Jesus Christ, the Buddha, and
many others in earliest history. In fact, we are told that the gods
themselves instructed humanity at the dawn of history, at which
time humanity was entirely conscious of the inner world and had
gradually to learn to become aware of the crystallizing Physical
Plane.

The gods, or those members of the hierarchy who are in charge
of the elements and the different forces of Nature, have always
been appreciated throughout the ages and worshipped in
excellent symbolical form by such people as the Egyptians, the
Assyrians and the Chinese. All these faiths in their original root
form acknowledged the One God over all. For instance, if we
study the revival of that pure religion as it was cultivated by King
Akhnaton, we will see that he founded it upon a former faith,
existing thousands of years previous to his time, which worshipped the one God.

We are told that humanity has had to pass through a long dark
Age of Materialism in which to learn to master physical matter by
its own means. This accomplished, it will rise once more from the
'Maya' or 'Illusion' of the importance of matter and focus its
eyes upon the real inner world of causes and realities.

Human beings were built originally, we are told, with a special
organ with which to register the *finer* vibrations of the physical
world, the realm of the ethers.

This organ was known, as we have said, as the 'Third Eye'. The
'Third Eye' is placed between the other two, at the root of the
nose, and has its seat near the Pineal Gland. It is said that the
earliest people of all used only that middle eye, and were known as

the Cyclops. We are told that during the embryonic development of the human species, at first man's only organ was one which he used to feel with, and to differentiate between heat and cold. In time this organ recessed, and the *first sense*, of touch, spread all

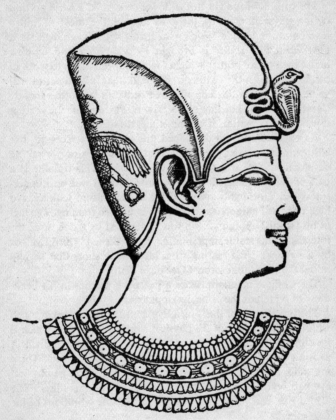

over the nervous system and through the skin. Apparently man's second organ to develop was his one 'Eye', which he used to see all 'non-solid' matter (which was all that existed at the time). As the earth solidified man developed his two physical eyes with which to view the solid world, and his second organ recessed, its etheric sight spreading all over the nervous system and having its seat in the solar plexus. It is said each of man's five senses will eventually spread all over his body in the same way.

The capacity for sight in the 'lower' non-solid etheric portion of the physical plane is therefore one of the most primitive involuntary functions, which man shares with the animals. It is only when this ability is brought by will-power and training under the control of man's higher faculties, and made to work in conjunction with the centres in his head, that it becomes of real value. Thus co-ordinated, all three activities are often loosely classed under the heading of the 'THIRD EYE', and for the present it will simplify matters if we sometimes do this also.

As physical eyesight developed, the etheric eye recessed, but although dormant at present in most people, it is only awaiting development and training to be reawakened. This training is a part of deliberate mystical development, which was well understood and thoroughly provided for in the ancient temples. No high ruler or Pharaoh was eligible without such training. The fact of his finished apprenticeship was announced by a nob upon the forehead of his statue, representing the awakened 'Third Eye', or by a serpent's head rearing from his own to show that he had raised the Kundalini serpent (*see* page 77).

The Chinese mandarin wore a peacock's feather in his head-dress to represent the same development.

The functioning of the 'Third Eye' puts the individual in touch with the greater part of the physical world, all that part which is invisible to the physical eyesight. The physical world is divided, as is all else, into seven interpenetrating planes or strata. These are solid, liquid, gaseous, and four kinds of ether. The physical eye can register or 'see' the vibrations of the first three. The 'Third Eye' can voluntarily register or 'see' the vibrations of the four ethers.

Certain creatures and types of activity (such as human beings and waterfalls!) have their final outer expression in solid form.

Many other beings and types of activity have their final outer expression in ether form or 'etheric matter' as it is called. For instance, we are told that the angels have an etheric body as their outer coat instead of a solid physical one as we have, and that this is because aeons ago, at the time when they went through the 'human' or individualizing stage, the ether was the densest condition of matter in existence.

When the 'Third Eye' is opened the individual begins to see all the manifold creatures and activities of the ether, and he approaches much nearer to the causes and realities of life. The mind can have power over everything which it can visualize. Therefore, while man is thus studying and learning to comprehend life in the ethers, he is able to develop the power to use and control some of this life.

He sees, for instance, exactly what his thoughts are and what happens to them. Once he has thoroughly comprehended the region of thought he uses and controls his thinking apparatus to much greater purpose.

He also studies the records of the earth's history which exist in the ethers in photographic form. He also gains an acquaintance with the plane described as the Fourth Dimension, the power to penetrate with one's sight or consciousness in every direction at once, and backwards and forwards through time.

Time and Space are physical attributes, but only an infinitesimal fraction of their limits can be apprehended by the senses while using their fleshly encasements.

The Yogi or Sage who wishes to know truth at first hand, and to study the workings of the universe, sets himself earnestly and patiently to reawaken his 'Third Eye' into activity, using timeworn and tested methods. He proceeds to study the conditions in each of the four ethers. He gradually accustoms himself to discriminate between and sum up the unaccustomed intricacies of interpenetrating, mobile and changing activities. The task is extraordinarily difficult and unimaginable to the ordinary man, but the Sage has access to instruction and help of which many of our less advanced mediums and psychics of the West are ignorant.

Truth is the essence of Purity, and therefore, as the Sage knows, can only be contacted by one of a like vibration.

Therefore the wise one acknowledges the first step to be the attaining of a condition of Purity—Purity of Motive and Purity of Living—a very little understood condition!

He next works to bring the brain under the complete subjection of his will instead of at the mercy of outside influences. By a series of carefully planned exercises he trains his mental equipment in much the same way as a dancer trains her muscles. The dancer gains complete control of her body at the cost of tremendous work and sacrifice. The Sage, for about the same cost of effort, gains complete control of the mind.

The mind is a very powerful instrument. We cannot say much about it at this juncture except that it can be compared with material of electrical constituency which has, if concentrated to one point, the same burning quality as fire. If a mind is divided upon several thoughts its burning force is dispersed in various directions. If concentrated upon one point it becomes as a burning-glass to the 'Sun' of its own Ego.

The effort of the Yogi, or any spiritual aspirant, is directed towards achieving one-pointedness of the mind. With this sharp instrument he can then bore through all the shells of illusion to the very truth and essence of all life. He can then deliberately wield and mould with his mind creative patterns which will help to shape the future. He is no longer confined to the haphazard creative efforts of the average man. He can create from the inside with the invisible sources of things.

With such capacities he can heal, prophesy and teach from the source of Truth. Such attributes the true Christian also is dedicated to seek, because they are the 'gifts of the Holy Ghost'.[1,2]

[1] Acts ii, 17.

[2] In 1958 a controversy in the Press has taken place regarding accusations levelled at Dr. Kuan, author of *The Third Eye*, in which details are given of an operation said to be performed by Tibetan monks for the purpose of producing the functions of the Third Eye. As these functions are also those of the 'Seven Gifts of the Holy Ghost', one might just as well declare it possible to have an operation on the brain to make one, overnight, into a good and fulfilled Christian! It is a question not of the physical tissue, but of heightened vibrations. Surely an unnatural operation of the kind described would belong in the realm of Black Magic.

To do these things, however, it is not enough to have opened the 'Third Eye', or the Eye of the Soul. This knowledge of the universe must be linked with the highest creative force within the body before creative activity can follow.

The seat of this creative force is in the throat, in the Thyroid gland. When the magnetism of the soul dominates the body it draws up reserve force from the base of the spine, where it was used for the animal nature, to the throat, as we mentioned in the description of the Kundalini serpent. This fire of creative force can then be used for inspired creative work of various kinds. But the highest expression of the power of the throat centre lies in the spoken word. God *spoke* and created the world. Christ spoke and called to the dying to arise and walk.

Man is a god in the making, and the goal is waiting before him. When once he has set his feet firmly upon the path of attainment his earnest aspirations will burn the dross out of his body and mind. Then by degrees the centres of force located within his seven major glands will be enabled to function. These centres, named by the Indians *chakras*, connect him with the knowledge of and power consciously to work in the different planes of matter.

Man's whole mentality can by this means be re-oriented and changed from a limited conception of third-dimensional objective life to a broad understanding concerning the why and the wherefore of the universe and his own part in the scheme of things. He achieves a telepathic union with the Mind of the Being whose body is this solar system, sometimes spoken of as Cosmic Consciousness.

The science of self-development along these lines usually includes special dieting, fasting, breathing and posture, but the principal aspect of this training is known as Meditation.

The practice of Meditation is creeping into various of the Western cults and occult societies, under different guises, and, alas, in some cases, in incomplete and misconceived forms. However, the germ of the idea has already taken root in the West, and as everything is speeded up nowadays it may come to be more quickly understood than we could expect.

The third factor which is necessary for this attainment of man is the heart. Sequestered in one of the ventricals of the heart is what is called the 'seed-atom' of man's physical body. It contains a minute image of the man himself, and his own body is said to be a large replica of it. This seed atom is the little record, the actual essence of the man's personality, the link or channel between him and his soul. It holds the 'silver chord' to the heart, and when it is severed and 'death' occurs the seed-atom leaves the body and is preserved in the subtler realms until the man's reincarnation, when he is formed from it again.

We can say, therefore, that the actual man himself, his real personality, his essence, his memory and all of him that will endure, dwells, in the last analysis, within the heart. For this reason all that man learns, through training and combining his physical brain with his higher mind, must be linked with his heart before it is really his. Christ said 'As a man thinketh in his *heart* so is he', and 'Where a man's heart is there will his treasure be'.

The function, action and quality of the heart is Love. Love in its broadest sense is the desire for reunion with the divine Spirit of the Creator which permeates all life. Love is the magnet which holds all life together. Its attraction is so strong that nothing can resist it.

Through the direct access of the heart to the Divine Spirit of Love or Truth come those 'intuitions' which are always more reliable than the 'thought-out' processes of the brain—everything which you can love you can undersatnd. Put limitations to Love and you limit life. That is what most of us do. We confine our love to one or two people and possessions, and close ourselves to the rest of life.

To reach the divine Truth, therefore, the heart must desire it, the heart must love it above all else. And then the power of the heart will link the man within it to his illumined mind and brain, the active Pineal Gland and Pituitary Body. The perfect Triangle will have been formed, the Triangle that has been drawn and symbolized and named in so many tongues.

Then the birth of the God in Man takes place—'Unless ye be

reborn . . .' We must quote the Christ in this connection because His great work, we are told, was to flood the earth permanently with His own great Spirit of Love, to make it possible for humanity to attain this rebirth of the Soul through the pure straight channel of the Heart alone. Since His coming it has no longer been necessary to have strict occult training and deep mental development before spiritual heights can be achieved. From then onwards the heart has been able to reach illumination through direct union, through love and worship, with the great Christ spirit, and through following the standards set by Its embodiment in the man Jesus.

The sacrifice of the Christ spirit in thus bearing the heavy mantle of earth vibrations in order to support the faltering heart-beat of humanity has been greater than we are able to imagine. Humanity would appear to be very slow in taking advantage of it, and seems hardly able seen to grasp the standards set for it as yet.

'Love thy neighbour as thyself'—so simple and so clear! and quite enough to change this tortured earth to a lovely place.

'Be ye wise as serpents and harmless as doves.' Here again we have the serpent as the age-old symbol of the Kundalini serpent which rises up the spine and links together the great Triangle. We can gather that Jesus Christ taught His disciples the science of Meditation. Often He took them apart into a high place (or plane). We read that one of them even reached the 'third Heaven' and learned there of things which no man is allowed to tell.

The Buddha sat in Meditation for years until he had gained access to the Universal Knowledge.

Such great spirits have done much of the preliminary work for us and have shared with us their knowledge, so all we need do is to profit by it.

It is not necessary for all of us to travel the occult path, to study deeply and to train as mystics. We are all at different stages along the 'Path'. We must not over-reach ourselves or we will have to retrace our steps. Many of us, in fact, may choose, sub-consciously, to continue with our most vital inner development only during our hours of sleep, and to withhold our growing knowledge, for the time being, from our little waking brain. But it is never too early for any of us to take the quickest way—to begin to learn to *Love*, and to clear out all the accumulated rubbish of false thinking, intolerance and greed which is robbing us of the Light of Life.

Whether we choose to approach the Truth through the discipline of study, complex thought and abstruse language, or through the discipline of self-sacrifice and service, the essence of that which we seek remains the same—too simple for words or brain, just a letting go of fear and ambition for the self.

We are trying to overcome habits of thought embedded in our personalities for centuries. For some of us this may only be possible at our present stage through the constant drilling of words, words, words! Others may be able to short-circuit them by a tremendous effort of Love.

But however the goal is approached, and however it is achieved, let it be borne in mind that the gate of man's deliverance, his birth as a god in human form, is heralded by the re-opening of the 'Third Eye', after which he will remain no longer blind to everything in life except the tiny excrescence which we call the physical World!

14

FIRST STEPS TO MASTERY

THE mastery of which we speak is a potent inner quality that may manifest outwardly in various forms, according to the decision of the Ego or Inner Man.

We are told that the Ego decides before birth upon the experiences, hardships and conditions of life by means of which it shall learn its next lesson, 'develop its next spiritual muscle', upon earth.

It then chooses, or is drawn to, a birthdate which will tune it in to such conditions, and selects parents with whom it had already built up certain Karma or obligations in former lives.

It is pointless, therefore, for the individual to try to shirk, avoid, or mitigate the experiences and difficulties of his life thus expressly selected to help him. To do so would be merely to postpone the issue and lose chances of development. The issue at hand is to learn a certain spiritual Law, to cure a certain defect in character, and to develop a certain quality of mastery. Therefore an intelligent man will strive to discover where he stands and what is the lesson he is required to learn. If he is then able, by an effort of will, to anticipate this lesson by deliberately training his heart and mind to the stage required, he may in this way obviate the necessity for an unpleasant experience.

Thus may a man learn to master his own stars, by eradicating in his character those vibrations which attract the analogous disciplinary stellar influences to him.

The individual may choose thus to hasten his development by speeding up the improvement in his own character. Or he may take the simpler way of the heart, the way of Intuition and Love. In this case he will, through opening his heart in love and faith, establish a direct link with the Great Plan, the joy of which super-conscious Knowledge will uphold him through all experience. It will illuminate his path through life, investing sorrows and joys with the radiance of their inner message, so that he would not wish one particle of his life changed. 'Stone walls do not a prison make'—nor do palaces make a paradise !

Illumined poets throughout the ages have expressed these truths. Milton said, 'The mind is its own place and in itself can make a hell of heaven or a heaven of hell.' We have to learn to taste life to the very dregs while listening intently for the inner spiritual message which it teaches, and never losing sight of the inevitable and glorious goal—Godhood.

The first step to mastery is, therefore, to put the mind in order, to train it to work clearly and dispassionately and to establish a true perspective on life. We must clear out from our minds quite mercilessly all the accumulated rubbish, so that we will have a clean free field in which to develop the marvellous latent powers which are our heritage. We must get rid of all 'inhibitions', all false values, uncertainties, indecisions, fussiness and restlessness, all those states which eat away the vitality of body and mind.

We have paid much money in the past to doctors and special-ists to analyse our bodies for us. Finding the results not quite satisfactory, we instinctively turn to the psycho-analysts and psychologists, paying them to analyse that which we begin to feel is the root of our troubles. All these men do what they can for us. because we have given them cause to believe that we do not care to hear the truth—namely that we could do much more for our-selves than they can do.

Worry, rush, noise, anger, fear and envy poison the system just as surely as if we took arsenic. If we err sufficiently in any of those ways we die; therefore, if we err in any lesser degree we are still injuring ourselves; even although death comes more slowly, we shorten our lives.

It is recorded that venom has been found on the tongue of a man in a rage exactly similar in its constituents to the venom of a snake. The same poison has been found to be generated in the body of an angry bull. Such venom would of course emanate in a fine form from the body of a vindictive and furious person, and act as a subtle poison to all contacting it. The story is told of the ward of a certain hospital for the wounded during the war in which an alarming percentage of the patients died. Investigations were pursued and it was discovered that the matron had been all her life a 'man-hater'. After her departure the death rate returned to normal. There is also recorded an experiment in which the breath of a person who was very much upset was caught in a test-tube and found to contain enough poison to kill a small rodent in a few moments.

The effects of people's emanations upon flowers, animals and children is often very noticeable.

Love and hate, then, have each their chemical form and action. It is obviously impossible for doctors or teachers to do us any permanent good until we learn not to poison ourselves and those around us.

The true spiritual qualities entirely eliminate these poisons.

Absolute faith makes fear and worry an impossibility. Unreserved love leaves no room for hate, anger, envy or greed. Worship of beauty in abstract and concrete form strengthens and protects man in all his activities. One who is able to live in this way needs no outside help and sheds warmth and radiance on all around him.

If we wish seriously to set the stage and prepare the way to this attainment our first step must be gradually to eliminate all unnecessary thoughts, desires and habits from our lives.

Every day for a few weeks we should examine ourselves thoroughly, writing down honest replies to the following questions:

(1) What are our ideals? In what do we really believe?
(2) What is our ambition in life—and *why*?
(3) Are we prepared to face the truth about ourselves and make a change? Or are we liable to sit on both sides of the fence?
(4) What are our faults? And what are our talents? What are we doing about them?

(5) What are the things which affect and worry us? Just how important are they?

This examination should be persevered with until all the answers are clearly written down. It will be found that so much sound thinking has probably never been done before. The result will be like a tonic to the brain and a stimulant to the endeavours. The important thing is to clear out everything from the mind which we can possibly do without, so as to concentrate all our powers upon the strictly necessary.

One of the Seven Devils of mankind is Possessiveness.

Possessions rule us while appearing to be our slaves. Our lives are cluttered up with possessions which we are sure that we need; they take up our time and money, tie us to places and complicate our lives in a thousand ways. To be continually looking at quantities of possessions confuses the brain. A clairvoyant gazes at the crystal merely to prevent her physical eye from seeing any objects; she knows that to see them detracts from the powers of the mind.

The Yogi discards all possessions, and tries to discover the minimum needs for physical existence.

Jesus Christ instructed His disciples to go out into the world to teach, taking only the barest necessities of raiment.

Possessiveness is the root cause of all wars, tyrannies and other obscenities. It is founded on an entire fallacy. If we endeavour to possess anything we at once separate that thing and ourselves from the rest of life. We are meant to possess all things, to share all things, to be a part of all life, to have power over all things— not over one. If we insist on striking always on one note the rest of the music is lost to us.

The desire to possess people or one person also defeats its own end, restricts progress and leads to jealousy—the gate of madness. We should respect the privacy and originality of every human soul and allow it complete freedom for development. Otherwise the inner spirit resents the outrage of repression and love dies.

Possessiveness arises from the innate unconscious knowledge that we are born to own and to unite with All; we must learn to transmute our petty physical possessiveness back to its divine origin. By this achievement a great amount of the unnecessary will be removed from our lives.

The next step is to study our own processes of thought. We will soon discover that we are usually 'thinking of a hundred things at once'. It would be impossible for several shorthand typists to capture all the thoughts which jostle one another through our brains in the space of a few moments. This shows that we divide the power of our minds up into about a hundred parts, giving only a very small portion of it to any one thing. Therefore we do most things with a tiny percentage of our actual capacity, which usually remains for ever unknown.

Once having eliminated all unnecessaries from our minds, we can give undivided attention to anything we do. The completely undivided attention of the mind is all-powerful, omnipotent, a force that can burn through everything and bend everything to its command. This is known to occultists, mystics, and students of these things, who spend the best part of their lives in practices and studies with this end in view.

In the West such training as Pelmanism coincides in many particulars with the Eastern traditions and can produce similar excellent results. It can safely be said that nothing in any sphere of life will be successfully achieved until the capacity for one-pointed concentration has been developed.

The third step in the preliminary process of self-analysis is to gain a clear conception of our sense of values and as concise an idea as possible of our definition of right and wrong, good and evil.

Many of us do not agree with the statements of the Christian Scientists that there is no such things as evil and that pain does not exist.

We feel pain, and we see evil and ugliness around us. Perhaps it would be more practical to accept the evidence of our senses and try to discover what part the dark side of life is meant to play in the scheme of things and how we can best co-operate.

A little thought will make clear that this world is built up in reality of a collection of opposites, and that it is only through being able to compare these opposites that we are able to have any views at all. Light would be meaningless to us if we did not know darkness; summer would be equally monotonous if we had no winter; warmth could not be appreciated if we did not suffer cold; peace and silence exist to us by reason of their contrast with noise; and goodness itself would be non-comprehensible were we not able to compare it with evil. Without sin and pain where would we be? 'Perfect', with no possibility of further progress, static!

If we are to evolve to something better on this earth, we must be given some means by which to do so. How should we be able to grow, to learn, to conquer, without such aids as sin, sorrow and pain? If the imagination is sufficiently alive to picture a world devoid of 'evil', life would be seen going round and round in a complete groove, without incident, without change, getting nowhere!

In the earliest days of the religion from which part of the Christian beliefs have sprung, Satan was worshipped. He was understood to be the greatest benefactor of man, placing before him temptations and experience without which he would remain stagnant and futile.

Without experience man cannot create. At present humanity is said to be evolving from a state of ineffectual virgin 'spirit' into self-conscious creative 'Godhood', and this is mostly through the help of 'evil' or 'Satan'. According to this, then, one can no longer call Satan 'evil', nor can one think of evil as evil if it is so beneficial to us.

It *is* possible, therefore, to say that there is no evil.

What, then, is there? What causes all the trouble?

There is only un-balance. Perfection is true balance of all the parts whether it be found in a human face, in character, or in the works of Nature. And this is where man's free-will comes in. He is able to upset the ideal balance of things by stressing too much some particular aspect. This upsetting of the balance at once creates a state of non-perfection or 'evil'.

Too much stress upon the possessive feelings, for instance, produces the 'sin' of jealousy.

Too much stress upon the bodily sensations produces a glutton or a libertine.

Too much stress upon mental sensations creates a crank or a fanatic.

Even if a man puts too much stress upon his spiritual side and ignores his body he may go mad—*unbalanced*, as it is rightly called.

There are many lesser stages of madness not recognized as such—a snob, a miser, a murderer, all expressing advanced stages of over-balance or the putting of too much stress on any one thing.

We all do this inevitably in one way or another, because of our free-will, and in order to learn the great law of Karma—cause and effect, action and reaction.

Satan was at one time called the Magistrate of God, the Keeper of Karma and of Numbers. His work was to stand by and deal out the lawful effects of unbalance. It can be imagined, therefore, that the glutton might be given a diseased body, lasting throughout several lives until he learns balance in that respect. The fanatic or the man who has ill-used, or not used, his brain might be given imbecility for a life or two, until he learns to understand the necessity for keeping a balanced brain. The theory seems to be that the soul of man, in these cases, chafes with impatience within his imbecile or diseased body, bewailing the wasted time due to his former foolishness, and developing good resolutions for the future.

It takes a long time for man to learn this simple law of cause and effect, and meanwhile he blames his parents, circumstances or Fate for his shortcomings. When he learns that he himself has been developing these shortcomings in former lives he can no longer blame his parents. Nor can they say that they have not deserved such a son, for he is their Karma as much as they are his!

Finally, we are told, man will master this lesson of balance—or non-evil—in all parts of his make-up.

He will learn to love deeply, but unselfishly, without stressing the self, understanding and forgiving all because of his own experience and realization of the laws of development. He will no longer give all his love to his own people and nothing to the world. He will realize that all the world is *serving* him—with the experience he so deeply needs for his growth. And he will keep the balance by giving back to the world always, giving of all the love and understanding he has, without criticizing that '*evil*' by means of which others are striving to develop, just as he is. Understanding the law of rebirth, he will realize that all stages, either of ignorance, sin, unhappiness or achievement, either have been or will be once his own. He will learn to balance his emotions with his aspirations, becoming dispassionately passionate, joyfully serious, calmly intense, unhurriedly quick, and actively passive.

To attain complete balance in the character self-study is necessary.

'Man, know Thyself' was inscribed over the doors of the wonderful ancient temples of learning as the most important injunction to all aspirants.

'The man who has mastered himself has mastered the world', is another well-worn saying, which gains in significance when we reflect that man is said to contain within himself a facsimile of and a link with everything in the universe.

Having thus set the stage mentally and physically for our progress to self-mastery, we can now outline the preliminary stages of the actual process.

The two most marked points in a person's life are the beginning and the end of his day, and it is to these, first of all, that we must give especial attention.

There is a certain exercise which is given throughout the world to all those who are seeking 'wisdom and perfection'. It is considered of primary importance, and like all exercises depends for its effect upon the regularity of its performance.

It consists of a careful *Review* of the events and actions of the day before going to sleep. The mind must travel slowly backwards through all the incidents, thoughts, motives, acts and words of the day, seeking quite impartially for traces of unbalance and also for traces of wiser understanding. Experience gained must be noted, and a frank and cool summing-up of failure and achievement must be made without either pride or condemnation.

This exercise, if faithfully and honestly repeated every night, will work miracles in the character. It performs two services of invaluable importance.

Firstly, it enables us to go through our Purgatory here and now as we go along, instead of waiting for its advent in accumulated form at some future date. By this means we can cancel out whatever particular 'Hell' we would have made for ourselves, as well as much earthly Karma. Our conscience, through being developed just like any muscle, will become so strong that in the end we will have as much difficulty in going wrong as formerly we had in trying to keep right. This is a fine way of clearing the decks for action, casting out much waste thought, remorse, and other exhausting inhibitions.

It will mean, also, that when we pass out of the body in sleep we can travel straight through to the heart of things, without being held back to the coarser realms by any tormented 'earthbound' thoughts. Our sleep will therefore be deeper and more refreshing. We will have a better chance to gain the 'soul-wisdom' and inspiration which true sleep brings. This exercise also helps to etch experience into the memory, thereby avoiding the need for a recapitulation of the events, and so saves much time for the developing soul.

The second of these vital exercises must take place at the moment of awakening. An effort of the will should be made to capture and remember the 'dreams' or experiences of the night before they rapidly fade from the memory. All that is recollected, however trivial, must be written down. After some practice valuable ideas, inspirations and even prognostications will begin to be remembered. The final result will be an unbroken train of consciousness during the twenty-four hours, which consciousness man will learn eventually to carry straight through the veil of death, and back with him at his next incarnation.

By means of these two simple exercises, the morning and the evening Review, he whose aspirations are high, sincere and enduring may begin at once to achieve his Godhood and acquire his first-hand knowledge of the secrets of the universe.

15

MEDITATION

'IT IS in silence that the soul speaks.'

Men have always realized the mystery of silence; they have ever been haunted by the feeling that silence and stillness are full of a potent and vital *Something* that is lost during activity and noise. 'Speech is silver but Silence is Golden', said the poet.

As we gain in experience we will be able to observe that one of the hallmarks of men great in spiritual qualities is that they are calm, still, and sparing of speech, although extremely vital. If you meet a man or woman of this type keep near to them. You will learn much from them, even without words.

The Science of Meditation has been used throughout the ages as the means by which a man can link his brain, mind and soul together, and connect them consciously with the Universal Intelligence—or the Mind and Motives of the Creator of this Solar System.

By means of Meditation man learns to concentrate and project his attention straight through the physical plane to the Fourth Dimension, then later to further dimensions. He endeavours to bring that which he learns through into the physical world, translated into physical language, and interpreted into his own brain as best he can. In the realms which he may reach, language, colour and form have quite different expressions to those with which we are familiar. He is getting to the heart of things, the underlying causes, the primordial truths which eventually give their faint distorted reflection as physical colour, sound and form.

He learns much that cannot be expressed in words or even in 'physical' thought. His brain must be gradually trained to encompass these unfamiliar aspects of life. Often this is well-nigh impossible, and, instead, the knowledge is absorbed and held by his 'super-conscious' mind. It feeds strength and stability into his character without his being conscious of the process at all. The result of this union with Divine Intelligence is that man can now work in accordance with the *Plan*; he is spared the tragedy of wasting his efforts in the wrong direction. That which he does and the influence which he spreads will be for the good of humanity—it will be a definite building up for future progress. The innate knowledge which he has thus acquired he may express in the creation of music, art, literature, a new 'religion', new economic or social developments, or else in an example of fine personal living.

He no longer needs to have faith in the existence of ultimate and divine realities. He *knows*. He has put himself in touch and in tune with them, and henceforth can bask inwardly in the radiance and joy of his knowledge. He can mentally look down upon the conflicting processes of the world's development, including his own little suffering, much as one would study a fascinating Chinese puzzle. With one part of him he suffers and experiences, while at the same time with the other part he enjoys, comments and learns.

To many people the attainment of such a state of knowledge and power has been all-important. They have given up their lives to it. Such people are the Yogis, Disciples, Buddhas, and those of their kind in all countries.

There is a fundamental difference between Eastern and Western peoples.

Those of the East draw everything inward to themselves and hold it, and are comparatively inactive although they learn much—intraverts.

Those of the West are full of action and energy, but give little time to studying themselves and acquiring deep knowledge before they act—extraverts.

So in the East we find inspired inaction resulting in stagnation.

And in the West we find uninspired action resulting in chaos.

When universal love, neighbourliness and brotherhood eventually spread across the world, East and West will learn from each other and pool their attributes.

The result will be Inspired Activity. We have already seen the earliest beginnings of this amalgamation around us. While Westerners are busy improving living conditions in the East, oriental teachers of philosophy and spiritual laws are gaining a considerable hearing in the West.

The ideal towards which we have to work is therefore Meditation followed by Action.

Let us now consider the actual process of Meditation and its several phases.

Imagine a great orchestra playing a powerful symphony. In the orchestra is one delicate muted violin, which we cannot hear although it plays all the time. The louder vibrations swamp its sound. If the louder instruments be stopped one by one the violin will still not be heard. Finally when they have all ceased we can suddenly hear it playing faintly. Our ears gradually accustom themselves to it until it appears to be making a volume of clear sound.

This is a good simile of the process of meditation. The human being is like an orchestra of varying vibrations. The louder, coarser vibrations are those of the atoms of body and brain. The finer are those of the emotions and thoughts. The muted violin represents the soul's message trying to filter through. To hear the soul's message all the rest of the orchestra must be silenced.

All the criss-cross currents of bodily sensations, thoughts, memories, hopes, desires and emotions must be stilled into complete passivity. Then the brain must be held poised and ready to receive the impress from the mind of that which the latter has been able to translate of the soul's message.

The soul is the ego's *intermediary* between the world of spirit and the world of matter, the storehouse of the results of experience in both realms, flashes of its knowledge coming to us as 'Conscience' or Inspiration. The soul has been likened to a mirror which can reflect the spirit world into the physical, but is usually too clouded over with vibratory disturbances to do so.

'Now we see through a glass darkly but then face to face.'

Meditation stills the vibratory disturbances of the personality,

and the mirror clears. The first stage in meditation is therefor
complete bodily relaxation. This cannot be accomplished whe
the body is in the wrong position. There are one or two posture
which have been proved to be suitable. The spine must be ered
and well balanced, and the ribs must be free for deep breathing

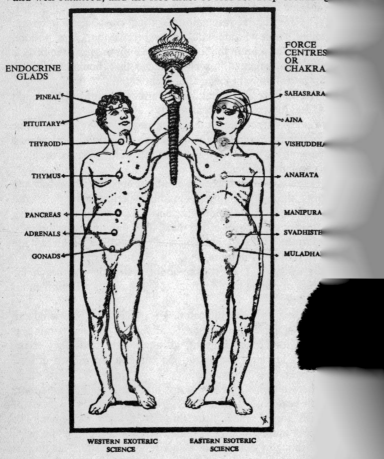

THE TORCH OF PROGRESS

The early Egyptians used to sit very upright upon a chair with
the eyes gazing straight ahead, the hands palms downwards
upon the knees, the elbows well tucked in to throw out the chest,
the heels together and the toes apart. They have left many
statues represented as meditating in this position. We are told it
is the one best suited to the Westerner also.

The Indians meditate mostly sitting cross-legged upon the
ground. Those who are skilled and expert use the 'Lotus' posture,
in which the soles of the feet are turned upwards and the body is
locked and balanced in such a manner that should the devotee
pass into a trance he cannot fall over.

The Chinese also squat, using various postures of the hands
and feet to achieve different results.

The Westerner who is making a beginning should adopt the
Egyptian pose, and learn completely to relax sitting upright, and
balancing the spine, neck and head so carefully that he ceases to
be conscious of them.

He must then commence to breathe deeply, silently, evenly and
slowly, through the nose, and gradually perfect this process until
he can perform it also unconsciously. The slower the breathing
the easier the control of the mind—but only that which can be
performed without the slightest effort or strain is of any use
whatever for his purpose.

By means of these two preliminary steps he has begun the
process of stilling the vibrations of first his physical and then his
etheric body.

His next and more difficult task is to tackle his emotional and
mental equipment. He must drop all *feeling*, all stress, strain and
desire for accomplishment, all anxiety or excitement at the
object in view. Excitement and emotion are formed of low,
heavy and 'noisy' vibrations.

There remains now the brain, that bustling little typewriter
which ceaselessly taps out the drifting or hurrying crowds of
thought-forms which float through it upon the ether. The
aspirant must patiently, continuously, and without effort, wipe
these thoughts out as with a sponge upon a slate. This process
must be continued until it can be performed unconsciously, a

difficult feat which may need months or years of practice. When, however, this has been accomplished the practice of Meditation becomes possible.

In some occult parlance we are told to 'make the mind a blank' for Meditation. These words lead to an entire misconception. If the ear is listening very intently for a certain sound, oblivious to all other sounds, we do not think that the hearing is a blank! On the contrary, it is actively at strict attention. So must the mind be, in Meditation, held at strict attention, ready to convey to the typewriter brain its interpretation of the impressions filtered through to it by the fine vibrations of the inner activities—the 'subtler planes where knowledge is'.

The best times for Meditation are said to be upon awaking and at about 6 p.m. It should be practised either before or several hours after a meal. The room should be dim or dark. The eyes should be facing a plain surface with, if desired, only one symbolical object on which to concentrate, or, if preferred, the eyes may be closed.

We have now described the condition to which the aspirant must learn to bring himself if he hopes to practice Meditation with any success.

The science itself is divided into four successive stages: Concentration, Meditation, Contemplation and Adoration.

Only the first two are possible to any but the adept or full-fledged mystic, nevertheless we will describe them all.

The process of Concentration has already been partly analysed. It consists in getting full control over the personality and then, when the aspirant's whole make-up is stilled and passive, in concentrating the attention of the brain to one point, keeping it clear, steady and empty of stray thoughts, waiting to receive the information which the mind is collecting.

When full Concentration has been established, then Meditation can begin. Meditation consists in studying with great thoroughness one object, subject, quality or force in life. As we have before stated the concentrated one-pointed mind is like a powerful burning-glass or magnet. When tuned in to the particular vibration of any object or quality it can burn right through to the truth of it and draw to itself everything connected with or of that same vibration.

BUDDHA IN MEDITATION.

Thus, supposing the aspirant has chosen a violin as the subject of his Meditation. He will first concentrate upon the violin, building up in his mind as vivid and complete a picture of the instrument as he is able. Then, holding the picture steadily before his mind's eye, he will begin to Meditate upon the instrument, endeavouring to learn everything he possibly can about it. He traces its history, the wood and other substances from which it was made, the process of making, the story of its design, its passage through the hands of dealers. Gradually it will be found that facts and information come to light of which the aspirant was hitherto unaware. That is the secret of Meditation—the possibility of actually learning without books, by active mental contact with the information sought.

The aspirant who wishes to learn of love, unselfishness, or the reality of the Divine Spirit, can reach this knowledge through meditating positively but not vaguely upon it.

Meditation can also be used to solve any of life's problems and difficulties. Simply state the problem in an absolutely dispassionate and impartial way, and wait steadily for the ideas relating to it to be drawn to the mind. A fair solution will almost inevitably arrive. The Oxford Group, now known as Moral Rearmament, use something of this idea for their 'Quiet Times'. Needless to say, a little knowledge is a dangerous thing. It is better thoroughly to understand what is happening, to avoid the danger of self-deception creeping in.

Meditation has to do with all the outer aspects and expressions of an object or quality—all its physical-plane attributes.

The third stage, Contemplation, has to do with the inner meaning, cause and Law behind any object or quality. In this case the mind ceases its activity and allows the subject of Contemplation to speak, to yield up its secret and reveal the mystery of its truth.

Having fully meditated upon the violin, if the aspirant could pass into the stage of Contemplation the envisaged instrument would disappear, leaving a space. Through that space would play the colours and forces of the subtler planes, those which form the Architype or Celestial pattern from which violins are made. The aspirant would learn the why and wherefore of a violin, its part in the evolutionary process and the actual creative quality of its particular tone. These things would come to him in a form of knowledge not clothed in words, and he would be at a loss how best to register and translate it for his physical use.

The fourth and last stage of this science is Adoration, and of this it is even less easy to speak.

Having learnt both the outer and inner meaning of his subject, the aspirant has reached to the core of it. He discovers the core of it to be the same as the core of himself—both spring from and are a part of the Mind of the Divine Creator. Having pierced through to this glorious and blinding realization, the aspirant can lose himself for a brief spell in the knowledge of that perfect Unity of Love. This is his moment of Adoration.

Through the steady practice of Meditation man can cease to be as a puppet dancing on the end of a string jerked by some unknown hand. He can learn to climb the string with his mind and will and take control of the hand. He can become the friend and associate of the Owner of the hand, and finally gain the freedom of complete identification with Him.

It must always be remembered when trying to describe non-physical states that physical language contains no suitable words or phrases. The unaccustomed brain must be presented with a simile only. When, through study or meditation, the brain has developed and adjusted itself the same truths can be presented in a more advanced manner which would not have been understood before. Therefore it is true to say that there is always much that is superficially incorrect in occult teaching, and in, for instance, such a book as this, because the neophyte brain must be coaxed along step by step, the pill of truth coated with the sugar of inaccuracy, until it becomes palatable in its pure form. However, books or no books, the truth is always there for those who desire it above all else.

Another type of work for those who wish to push forward is Group Meditation, or the blending of a small group of people to meditate in unselfish brotherhood together.

Inasmuch as this calls for the breaking down of many of the barriers that exist between the nicest of people—barriers of self-consciousness, intolerance, criticism, and egocentricity—it is obviously a very fine practice.

Christ said, 'Where two or three are gathered together in my name, there am I in the midst of them,'[1] thus pointing out that unity is strength on spiritual as well as on physical levels.

It may be inquired whether prayers do not suffice instead of Meditation. Prayers are the five-finger exercises, the A B C of spiritual growth. As such they will for ever play their part. But he who is not content to remain spiritually in the nursery will sooner or later require to put himself more individually in touch with the realities.

'St. Matthew xvii, 20

16

HISTORY OF THE WISDOM

BOTH the Bible and the history book, while being compiled for us, have passed through intensive censorships, besides suffering at the hands of unenlightened translators.

The result is that our orthodox education, both in religion and history, is often very misleading, and keeps us in complete ignorance of large and vital aspects of humanity's evolution.

Much of the records of the knowledge to which we would like to have access has been carefully guarded, secreted and even destroyed during periods when it was considered more expedient to keep the people in ignorance.

Nevertheless, there is still a wealth of literature all over the world awaiting the explorer. If he pursues his inquiries with patience and discrimination the following points will come to light.

The history of this earth is infinitely older than the modern historian admits. There exist many and various sects, orders, and religious and philosophical fraternities, who all possess exhaustive records and treatises describing the evolution of man upon this planet, and of the part that our Solar System plays in the Cosmic scheme.

If the pure and original root of these different beliefs can be uncovered, it will be found to be identical in most respects. In each case we will discover that the One God over all was acknowledged, and that the existence of the Hierarchy was well understood, and was tabulated and represented under the names of various gods and goddesses, nature-spirits and demons. The seven Great Spirits, their colours, attributes and elements, the seven planes and man's sevenfold bodies were all carefully studied and analysed. The great Cosmic Cycles and Periods, as ruled by the Signs of the Zodiac and all the astrological influences, both psychic and chemical, were subject to intensive research. The laws of Rebirth and Karma were embodied in all these beliefs.

We find that at the zenith of their civilization the various great ancient nations had perfected this knowledge and by its means produced immortal monuments to their science, such as the Great Pyramid. It transpires that such a golden period in the history of a nation was followed by crystallization, stagnancy, degeneration and a final breaking up, leaving only distorted misunderstood relics of the once-great knowledge. We learn that such great cycles were said to occur regularly under astrological influences which provide for the continual recommencing of man's lesson on a higher turn of the Spiral of Evolution, so that his development becomes ever subtler and more complete. Before each new surge forward of enlightenment man must be borne down within the crouching wave and submerged in darkness and ignorance.

In all these records reference is made to the wonderful Golden Age which occurred on the continent of Atlantis, which was said to have submerged during its proceeding period of degeneration. Mankind was said to have been taught the Ageless Wisdom by the gods themselves upon Atlantis, and to have carried its remnants with them in all directions as they fled to safer land. The story of Noah and the Ark is repeated in many tongues and in not very varied guise.

The Atlanteans were said to have founded the Egyptian culture and to have built the Sphinx, and their descendants the Pyramid. It is believed that the early Egyptian religion thus founded was the father of all the faiths which spread across Europe and Asia, as far north as the Esquimaux and the Laplanders, and as far east as China and Japan. In South America also perhaps the greatest of Atlantean colonizations took place, but at a still earlier date.

There have been at least 300 books written about Atlantis. The remains of its root language are said to be found in identical form among the Welsh, Irish, Basques, Western Spanish, and on the Canary Islands, Azores, Easter Island and in Mexico; as well as certain practices and beliefs. The Druids of England were believed to be the descendants of Atlanteans who built Stonehenge and other little-understood monuments in the British Isles.

We find also that a realization and consciousness of the inner realities was the prerogative of ancient man all over the world even if he lived as a barbarian. He did not need to *believe* in an after-life and a world of spirits. He *knew*. He saw 'ghosts', and he understood their difference from spirits. He communed with his dead. He knew of the nature-spirits, who ruled the elements; he understood their qualities, colours and their prototypes among the animals; he used animal effigies to represent them.

The Zuni Indians prayed to seven great nature-gods by means of the seven colours painted on their prayer-sticks.

The Tibetans also pray in accordance with colours, and designed different-coloured masks embellished with a large third eye for their 'devil-dances'.

In New Guinea the doctors paint their patients with the colours of the particular Spirits needed to effect a cure.

The Early Britons painted themselves with the colours needed to stimulate their prowess.

The colour of the Spirit of Darkness was usually black, of Light, white; of water and vegetation, green; of air, blue, and of fire, red. There was always the one Great Spirit over all whose colour was Golden.

In Egypt Horus was white, Osiris black, Shu red, Amen blue, and Num green.

The Egyptian Wisdom was brought to a high point under Ptah in the Temple of Memphis.

Wise men and students travelled from all over the world to study with the Egyptian priesthood, whose famous pupils included Moses, Jesus and Pythagoras, it is said.

The Egyptians named, described, and drew man's seven bodies, and went fully into all his activities after death. They understood the etheric, astral, mental and spiritual planes, also purgatory, paradise and the successive heavens.

In their renowned collection of pictures and writings called the *Book of the Dead* most of their beliefs are set forth. They considered each human being as living with one goal in view, that of perfecting his character in earthly life in preparation for his journey through the 'nether' world or astral planes, and his gradual progress through the subtler planes to 'paradise' or the heaven-world, helped by the various workers and representatives of the spiritual hierarchy.

The greater part of the Egyptian consciousness was concentrated upon the Path of Attainment and the evolution of mankind. By means of astronomy and astrology they mapped out a wonderful and stupendous panorama of the Plan of Evolution and the history of the world.

They originated the belief in the Messiah, whom they called the Ever-coming One. He was the Egyptian Jesus, called Iusa or Horus, and was reborn every 2500 years, or every time the earth passed into the next Sign of the Zodiac. During each of these great two-thousand-year periods He embodied the quality, lesson and type of the Sign. For instance, under the Sign Leo, Iusa or Horus was worshipped as a young lion and it is probable that the Sphinx was raised in his honour. He was born as a Scarabaeus in Cancer 10–12,000 years ago, in which Sign was also the crib or manger Star, and that of the Ass. During that period the scarab was worshipped. During the Sign of Taurus the Bull. He was born and worshipped as the Golden Calf. During the Jewish Dispensation He was reborn as a Lamb in the Sign of Aries the Ram. And finally in the Christian Era in the Sign of Pisces the Fish He came as the Jesus Christ of the New Testament. The Sign of Jesus was a fish, which is still engraved upon the Pope's seal ring; the Early Christians were known as the Pisciculi.

The cross was used 7000 years ago in Egypt to represent the power that upholds the human soul in death. The story of Jesus, of the Annunciation, the virgin birth, of His baptism, temptation, teaching, miracles, disciples, the Last Supper and His resurrection, had all existed and been elaborated in Egypt for 10,000 years.* Apparently it was merely adapted by the writers of the

* *Ancient Egypt the Light of the World* by Gerald Massey.

New Testament and modelled on to the life of the new and greatest Messiah, with certain alterations which clouded some of its deepest meaning.

There is only space to touch on this interesting subject here, which can be studied at the student's leisure.

Each of the great ancient religions had its Book of Records and Teachings, which were for the outer ring of students. This Book was always supplemented by a *Commentary* written for the inner circle of the priesthood, explaining the secret symbolism of the Book and the Mysteries therein concealed. Sometimes there was a second and third Commentary giving the deepest inner meanings. These Keys or Commentaries were carefully guarded and hidden, and in many cases have apparently disappeared altogether.

The ancient Indian philosophy began with the Veda, including the Upanishad books and their great Commentaries. The Rig and Yajur Vedas are some of the earliest records of Aryan thought. They come between the Egyptian and the Greek civilizations, and are assigned to about 5000 B.C. They worshipped a Heavenly Father (Dyans-Pitar) and spirits controlling the elements. They had a very deep conception of the One God. The Indian book of moral code, called the Laws of Manu, taught continence and moderation and the striving for a spiritual 'second birth'. All ten of the Indian philosophies taught Reincarnation.

Shankara, born about A.D. 788, was the great Indian saint and elucidator of the Upanishads. He wrote one of the world's masterpieces, his commentary on the Brahman Sutras, the Upanishads, and his 'Song of the Lord' (the '*Bhabavad Gita*)'. He was a great adept in Yoga.

Yoga is not a religion. It is a science, a method of 'yoking' up with the 'Supreme Self', a practice of extreme discipline for the attainment of perfection. A Yogin is one who has studied Yoga, often at the Buddhist University of Nalanda.

The Buddha was the great Indian mystic, founder of Buddhism. The Buddhist philosophy is based on the law of Karma. The Brahmins believed Buddha to be the reincarnation of

Vishnu, their ancient Teacher. They absorbed his teachings, which also took hold in Tibet, China, and in Japan among the Zen monks.

The Tibetans have also a *Book of the Dead* containing the 'Bod', which is a guide-book to the dying during the forty-nine days which constitute the 'Intermediary Stage' between death and Union with the Divine. Passages from this book are read to the deceased for forty-nine days after his death, while he is supposed to be passing through the three lower astral planes and viewing the panorama of his created thought-forms. He finally realizes illusion and craves a new rebirth. He is exhorted to believe in the One great Divinity of whom he is a part.

In Persia a very fine philosophy was cultivated. This was the Sufi with its book the *Avesta*. This was built upon a very early worship of the sun-god Mithra, which at one time held great sway in Europe as well as upon the teachings of the prophet Zoroaster.

The *Rubaiyat* of Omar Khayyám is inspired by Sufiism. The Sufis find ecstasy through losing themselves in union with the One Divine Spirit. Some of the Fakirs and Dervishes are their offshoots, but these are sometimes degenerated.

The Mohammedans possess a great wealth of philosophy in their book the Koran, which also teaches an aspiration to unity with the One God.

In China the religion, whether Buddhist or Taoist, is built upon the teachings of Confucius. Confucius was a very practical teacher and social organizer. Born in 551 B.C., he worked to develop social science and the building up of individual character, and did much to bind China together. He was almost a contemporary of Buddha, and was greatly influenced at one time by Lao Tze. His pupils recorded his teachings in a book called *The Digested Conversations*, a large part of which was burnt later during the Ts'in dynasty, with the usual object of keeping the people in ignorance. Confucius believed in the one God over all, and in three types of subsidiary spirits. He called himself the 'transmitter of the wisdom of the Ancients'.

Lao Tze was the Chinese 'Jesus'. He was born of a virgin

mother, conceived under a falling star. He was a high mystic and left a famous book called *Tao Teh King*, which expounded a moral code for the Way of Attainment. 'Tao' means Way and represents the aspiration of the Taoists. Lao Tze believed in Reincarnation, Karma, and the victory of gentleness.

The Japanese State religion was Shinto. Shinto means the Way of the Spirits. Some of the Japanese became Buddhists, and nearly all of them became Confucians as well.

Then there was a very stern type of Buddhism called Zen which gained great sway in China and was finally transplanted to Japan. The Zen classic is a poem called 'The Taming of the Bull', the bull being of course the animal nature or materialism. The Zen monks originated ju-jutsu, which has a deep scientific and mystical origin, and was practised by their famous samurai warriors.

The Greek philosophies, founded by Pythagoras, Plato and others, upon the Egyptian teachings, accepted rebirth and other of the ancient doctrines.

The Jews have their own great book of ancient records called the Kaballah, and the inner meanings of these writings were sought and studied by the famous Alchemists of the Middle Ages.

The Christian Church, as founded in Rome, guarded many priceless manuscripts. It accepted Reincarnation and Karma, as it said that Christ had also done.[1] But from the first General Council of Christendom at Nicaea in A.D. 325, to the last Council in Constantinople in A.D. 869, Christian principles, rules and teachings were subject to many deletions and changes. The result was to decrease public knowledge for the aggrandizement of the priesthood. From that time onwards all who possessed or were teaching the Secret Wisdom were mercilessly persecuted and put to death.

Henceforward the occult sciences were studied in secret. They were guarded and kept alive by such people as the Freemasons, Rosicrucians, Alchemists, Troubadours, Knights of the Grail and the Round Table, and the Avengensies or paper-makers. In

[1] St Matthew xvi, 13, and St. Matthew xvii, 12–13.

Russia there were the Trottes, and in Britain there had been the Druids. Earlier still, in Mexico, there were the remnants of the teachings of Quetzalcoatl, and of the ancient Atlantean settlement at Peru. In Chaldea there were the Magi or Magicians, the famous astrologers who possessed the Egyptian Wisdom and knew of the time and place where the new Messiah should be born. And in Palestine itself the wise ones belonged to the sect called the Essenes, which had existed for 8000 years, and was to have the privilege of training Jesus.

Everywhere in the world the self-same Ancient Wisdom can be traced, until its widespread stamping out and persecution at the beginning of the Dark Ages from which we are now emerging.

And everywhere in the world at present are the signs of the re-emergence of that Wisdom back into the light of day, not as the prerogative and secret of the priesthood, but as the hard-earned right of the whole of humanity. The tables have indeed been turned, and now we find much of the Wisdom outside the churches and temples instead of inside them.

Humanity is taking its salvation into its own hands. That is because we are now coming into the great Aquarian Age under the Sign of the Zodiac Aquarius, which will last, as do all the Signs, for about 2000 years. During this time the 'Waters of Life will be poured down on all mankind', and the astrological influences will bring a golden age to birth. Many believe that the Ever-Coming One will arrive again in His newest guise, which we may not yet know; but great will be the fulfilment for those who are ready and awaiting His Coming.

17

THE PRESENT AWAKENING

HAVING taken a lightning and very superficial survey of the history of the Ancient Wisdom, we can now trace the evidences of its resurrection at the present time.

The first steps were taken towards the end of the nineteenth century. H. P. Blavatsky contributed greatly by her inspired researches among ancient documents and the treasures she brought to light and so tirelessly analysed. She founded the work which has since been carried forward by the Theosophists and which consists of a modernization of some of the Ancient Doctrines, together with public instruction in the form of lectures and libraries. Various other teachers and communities too numerous to mention here have come forward all over the world to add their quota to the widespread interest.

Some of these stress the mystical side, some the occult, and some the practical. Everywhere there is a banding together of earnest people thrilled with their particular fraction of the un-earthed wisdom, each little group usually convinced that it possesses the one and only truth and way of salvation.

For a long time progress has been hampered by the old feeling of separatism and the intolerance of another's method of approach to the truth. But even that handicap is finally beginning to be overcome. The cry for world-wide unity, peace, brother-hood and the casting down of barriers is increasingly making itself heard.

The League of Nations points the way, however imperfectly, to the future welding together of the nations.

Such a movement as the Oxford Group[1] appears to be inspired, in spite of handicaps, to work for the future fusing of all classes in a common Christian spirit.

Fraternities like the World Fellowship of Faiths have fought

[1] Now "Moral Rearmament".

against almost insuperable odds of intolerance and stagnation, to draw together the religions of the world and bring to light their fundamental sameness. Groups have been formed all over the earth for purposes of spiritual propaganda, united meditation, and training for the selfless service of healing and harmonizing by thought and prayer.

The word 'international' is now so much in use that it is almost becoming a household word. Humane societies for the prevention of cruelty of all kinds are also doing valuable work and gaining increasing support, while education and health culture are being revolutionized.

Nudist movements, vegetarian and nature-cure practices, biochemistry and the latest method of psycho-analysis, all point the way to the future universal 'Yoga' of physical attainment which is being ushered in.

The promised individualization of the Aquarian Age is already in evidence. No newspaper can hope for success unless it provides crossword puzzles or competitions, or in other ways allows its readers to contribute each his own quota of self-expression or effort.

No film star dare run the risk of ignoring the individual outpourings and demands of his fans.

From the lowest grades of humanity to the highest can be seen signs of an increasing independence, self-consciousness and awareness.

It is true that at the present time the world is racked in parts by wars and bound down by oppression and dictatorships and that much cruelty and selfishness is in evidence. But these very activities are a proof of the restlessness and striving among all ranks, the stirring up of the mud in the pond before it can be cleaned. It is like the final orgy of a drunkard which precipitates the violent reaction through which he is able to regenerate.

The urge to combat stagnation and to struggle out of the ruts of convention and go forward no matter how has been evidenced for some time past in the adventures into 'modern' art, 'modern' literature, 'modern' music, and even 'modern' manners and morals.

All these signs are healthy and promising and only await the leadership of those who have put themselves in touch with inner realities to bear rich fruit.

One world-wide group of people, the 'Men and Women of Goodwill', are pledged to contribute that leadership in all phases of human living, fired by a lofty ideal of brotherhood which remains completely non-partisan and all-embracing. They are introducing an international periodical to foster the expression and reciprocity of goodwill all over the globe. This will be an advance on the hundreds and hundreds of periodicals already in circulation which are each solely concerned with the activities and teachings of their own little esoteric fraternity.

A deeper understanding of the arts and sciences is being taught by the schools founded by Rudolph Steiner, whose very name is an inspiration to students of the occult.

And so the work grows on all sides. There are some, of particular gifts, who are practising alchemy itself, revising the ancient mystic knowledge and probably preparing a wonderful step forward for medical science.

Others are working faithfully and steadily to spin a web of constructive thought across the world by the formation of groups everywhere meeting regularly in Meditation.

In the Church itself many are beginning to feel the fires of inspiration rising once more, and their congregations are quick to appreciate it.

Even those courageous ones who seek to expose the 'shortcomings' of the medical profession are met half-way by many of the doctors themselves.

The flame of regeneration and renaissance is burning high already, and many are the little sparks, fanned by patient souls, ready now to flare into a rich fulfilment.

We find too that a higher type of teaching is gradually permeating various centres of investigation both spiritualist and Christian-Scientist, occultist and psychic, a type of teaching which is insensibly and subtly drawing them all closer to each other. At the same time the materialistic scientist, chemist and experimenter is, by virtue of his very persistence, approaching to the self-same heart of Truth in his own way.

A wonderful era may soon dawn when humanity will figuratively rub its eyes to find that blinkers and barriers of so many kinds have somehow melted away and that it has learnt to turn its back upon the illusion of Division, and seeks only to unite and fuse all people and all activities into one coherent Whole which ever becomes simpler and more complete.

18

DANGERS IN THE PATH

HE WHO seeks Truth, the Philosopher's Stone, and is determined to uncover and master the secrets of the universe for himself, is treading a Path beset with many pitfalls, dangers and illusions. The weakest points in his character, the tiniest chinks in his armour will be cunningly assailed.

Honesty is the talisman which will enable him to reach and to recognize Truth—plain honesty about himself, his purpose, and other people.

Seekers are side-tracked mainly by two things, a love of sensationalism and laziness, both of which undermine their honesty. It must always be remembered that sensationalism (or emotional excitement) is to the mentality what sexual over-indulgence is to the body. Even religious emotion can be a type of mental sensuality, and therefore unbalancing.

The discovery of Truth is the most wonderful, powerful and helpful work that any human being can undertake, and the capacity to understand it is the greatest attribute which the mind can cultivate.

To attain this inestimable reward of wisdom, man must expect and be eager to go through at least as much discipline, study and restriction as he would endure while learning the piano or training as a boxer.

He must remember also that in the uncovering of Truth there is never a last word, nor a completely accurate statement about any particle of it, because neither the human language nor brain can encompass it. Truth to anyone is only that much of it which he can as yet understand. At a certain stage even an untruth may be taught. For instance, primitive nations had to be given a jealous god of war, until they evolved sufficiently to accept a loving god of peace.

The mind must be trained, just like a muscle, to cope with certain conceptions, and this very training enlarges and expands the capacity to understand still more. After a period of such training one can explain to an intelligent person something which he would have been quite incapable of visualizing at the beginning of it. It would have been impossible to talk of wireless, the telephone or gramophone to a man 200 years ago; neither his brain nor language was equal to it—he was living in the Dark Age. But to one of the wise priests of Egypt living 10,000 years ago one could have talked of these inventions and probably obtained a few suggestions! To understand the fundamental truths of life is to understand all! Those are the truths which Christ said would 'make us free'.

The first effort of the seeker, then, must be to avoid laziness and to love honesty and discipline.

When once we are attuned to this ideal we will be enabled to distinguish a wise and good person from a charlatan and so avoid an infinite number of disillusions and dangers. The hall-marks of the wise are easily distinguished.

Wisdom gives humility, peace, poise and strength; its owner ceases to be afraid, to be rushed, sickly, worried, ambitious, emotional, sentimental or changeable. His voice is resonant, neither shrill nor grating, and his presence is never exhausting.

A truly wise one will be sparing of words, nor will he loosely speak of initiations, Masters, visions, guides, or his own powers. People who talk of these things are childish—they have not felt the awe and reverence which first-hand knowledge gives.

A wise one will never ask money for teaching spiritual things; it is against the Law. He will have reached the stage where money sufficient for his needs comes without the asking. Nor will he ever try to persuade anyone to do or to think anything, nor will he attempt to teach unless earnestly asked to do so; for he has learnt to have the greatest care for another's free-will. A Wise one seldom uses the word 'I'.

He will never attack anyone, or any cause, yet he is full of strength and energy. He has learnt to be 'wise as a serpent and harmless as a dove'. He is not a crank on any one subject. He has become such a reservoir of love and of constructive thought that he is a worker of 'White Magic', lucky to those around him and the bringer of 'miracles' to pass.

Such a one is he who has for some while faithfully trodden the Path of Discipleship which leads to Godhood. He passes unnoticed among all those who are not seeking with the same purity of motive, the same vibration, as his own. He is sometimes very cleverly áped by the charlatan, or he who tries to serve both God and Mammon, the worker of 'black magic', the bogus 'Spiritual Teacher'.

This latter is usually very attractive to others. He has a strong personality, and often arouses extreme love and devotion in the people around him. This is because such a one has accumulated throughout many lives, because of his energy, the experience, vitality and power which he can now use for either good or evil. A very evil person is potentially a very good one. (It is the stored power which counts and which gains a hold on people. That is why the enterprising lost sheep is of more importance than all who stagnate meekly in the fold.)

If a charlatan spiritual teacher were to give himself up finally wholly to good he would gradually defeat his own personality and lose, one by one, those habits and ruts of thought which give him what his friends would call his 'little ways', those very human attributes.

A person who poses as a highly evolved being, a teacher of others, and yet has human habits and frailties, makes a tremendously strong appeal, because his achievement, apparently, needs little discipline and rigidity. For that reason his followers are eager to adore his personality, and he allows, against the Law, such adoration. Thereby he feeds his own vanity and their attachment to physical form. They are not encouraged to discriminate, but to believe blindly what he teaches them. And the 'teacher', once this blindness is established, encounters no spur of criticism or judgment to keep him to the giving of his best. So the little community soon becomes a sham and intellect retires.

The inevitable result of this situation is that a hypnotic condition arises, due firstly to the teacher's desperate desire to keep his followers' attention fixed only upon himself, so that they will not discover better things outside and cease to contribute to his sustenance; and secondly to the wish of his followers to give themselves up to the lazy, emotional state of adoring a physical personality, believing in wonders without the use of intelligence, and flattering themselves with the importance of possessing a 'great Teacher'.

This situation can frequently be met with. It is an ambitious imitation of the real thing, and because of a lack of honesty on all sides, it goes rapidly downhill. The combination of personality-worship, sensationalism and hypnotism soon leads these people into the toils of emotional, sensual and sexual indulgence of all kinds. Fraudulence, destructiveness, perversion and intellectual distortion flourish in this soil, and the link with the higher mind is broken. It was in such foundations that the horrible Black Mass and the orgies of 'black magic' were able to take root.

Black magic is simply the use of the developed mind-power for a wrong purpose. It exists in ratio to the strength of will and intelligence of the person using it and the lack of such in the victim or victims.

Any desire for power over others for either good or bad reasons is an act contrary to the great Law which stipulates complete free-will. The moment such power is established, we have a state of hypnotism, in slight or intense form, and therefore a condition of 'black magic'.

Black magic is not a thing of the past; it is a manipulation of natural laws. It is with us always, existing for instance in such groups round charlatan teachers as have just been described; existing sometimes side by side, almost hand in glove, with White Magic.

Rasputin was a typical example of a modern Black Magician, and I can think of other living examples who could also be listed in this category.

All such groups provide interesting psychological studies. The author personally knows of several. In one, the 'teacher', a woman, claims to be the reincarnation of one of the Apostles of

Christ. This is earnestly believed by a worthy but hypnotized little troop of women followers, who are blind to the fact that their 'spiritual leader' breaks most of the commandments under their very eyes. Another group is headed by a man who claims and is eagerly believed to be the reincarnation of three famous people in one! There are, I understand, several different 'reincarnations' of the famous Rosicrucian Comte de Saint-German alive at present, each supported by his little group! In fact, up to date the author has been honoured by the acquaintance of quite an array of 'reincarnated saints and historical celebrities'!

There are also, I am told, certain coloured teachers claiming the highest spiritual status, of whose relations with their white women disciples it would be better not to inquire, the hypnotized women believing themselves to be nearly as honoured as the 'Chosen of the Lord'; sometimes even with an acquiescing husband in the background.

All these things are going on, comprising an almost inextricable mixture of 'good and evil'. The wise seeker will learn to understand the necessity for it all, and wade through in safety, protected by the life-belt of his own pure motives. He will not turn in dislike or disapproval from those leaders who savour of charlatanism or incompetence. They each have their audiences, who are drawn to them because of similar vibrations, and could go, at their particular stage, nowhere else.

Sometimes good teaching comes from very faulty people. This fact is a means of stimulating students into recognizing truth for itself, as apart from a personality. On the other hand a person who is intrinsically good and true may be unable to utter a word of sense to satisfy a seeker, nor take any interest in his seeking. The world is full of infinite variety, and all are seeking and learning in their different ways. It is hard to know who fundamentally is the most 'advanced'. When the aspirant can understand this and grow to love his neighbours for their struggles and faults, and utterly abstain from any critical feeling, then 'will all things be added unto him'. There will be no barriers to prevent it. Like attracts like, and his own honesty and charity will inevitably draw to him as to a magnet all that is good.

By the same token, any weakness which still remains within his character will attract him to that with which it has affinity. If he has a latent tendency to accept too much from others, and to lean on them, he will be an easy prey for a certain type who bind people to them by a great show of generosity. If he finds himself saying, 'The one thing I cannot bear is meanness—I do like a generous character!' let him reflect that possibly he still has something of the parasite within him, and is not determined to be self-reliant. Let him beware lest he is captured by one who has learnt how much it *pays* to be generous and how easy it is by that means to get some people completely under one's influence.

Sometimes a 'teacher' who preaches and practises 'generosity' will soon obtain financial help from those well-meaning seekers who are able to give it, and will then proceed to gain more adherents by being generous with other people's money! This very real abuse is often put into practice, the final result being that much money which would otherwise be given to the poor is spent for the pomp and comfort of the 'teacher' and his somewhat nebulous 'cause'.

A genuine teacher always deserves and usually gains support but his 'pomp and circumstance' is conspicuous by its absence.

The final warning which must be given is about the imagination. By this word I refer to that power which the mind has to form images of that which it desires, and which it uses more successfully subconsciously than deliberately and consciously. There is a tremendous, intricate and forceful world of subtle life lying just below the threshold of the conscious mind which can be manipulated to produce varied results.

For instance, we sometimes hear of an earnest emotional female who has been practising either 'meditation' or 'psychic development' not wisely but too well, describing a wonderful vision she has had, perhaps of the 'Christ Himself'. Who possibly spoke words of praise to her. She becomes vastly important and ecstatic about the vision, and her friends are much impressed.

But what really happened?

To begin with, the lady by affirming such an experience gives away at once her complete ignorance as to what is possible in such a way. In all probability that which occurred was simply a case of 'imagination', self-hypnotism into seeing and hearing that for which she longed; or she may perhaps have picked up the thought-form of someone else's imagery. In any case, the one thing certain is that if anyone were sufficiently 'advanced' to obtain a genuine spiritual experience they would be so filled with awe and so alive to the laws pertaining to such experiences that they would find it quite impossible to say a word about it. The only sign of it would be a radiance emanating from them to those who were sufficiently sensitive to feel it. The great Moses, after having talked with the Lord, was obliged to veil his face because it shone so much that the people could not bear to look upon it.

Imagination can play us many tricks, but we can test things out pretty safely in the following way. Any experience we may have which makes us want to 'tell' about it is not the real thing, but something to which we have laid ourselves open through an unconscious wish for a thrill or to acquire importance. Of a real experience we will never wish to speak, because we will realize intuitively that each soul grows at its own pace, and that our vision was sacred to us alone. The resulting faith that we enjoy is all we will impart. Therefore we must never be impressed by any idle and emotional talk we may hear about these things.

It is important, however, to try to visualize the condition of that invisible envelope of 'compressed ether' (for want of a better description) which surrounds us and goes by the name of our 'aura'. This contains a vast panorama of photographs, 'astral talkies' of all our memories both conscious and forgotten. When we are forced slowly out of our bodies in drowning we see this aura ourselves, and review a rapid panorama of the events of our lives, as has often been attested.

Anyone who is genuinely 'clairvoyant', such as a crystal-gazer or fortune-teller, is able to see this aura on approaching us, and can pick out pictures of past events, as well as those of our sub-conscious hopes for the future, and therefore describe intimately our dead relatives or our home life—almost as easily as we could describe any film we were watching! There is not necessarily anything wonderful, new or valuable for us to hear—merely that which is already there attached to the mind.

Sometimes, however, she may even get a correct picture of some future event. In this case she is probably reading a thought-picture in our aura which we brought through subconsciously from something we were allowed to learn of in a dream. For those who are tempted to explore the phenomena of clairvoyance it is very necessary to study the human make-up from the psycho-analytical point of view, otherwise it is easy to be rendered awe-struck by some occurrence for which there is a scentific explanation.

The world is indeed full of many astonishing conditions and activities. It is better to have a clear understanding of anything untoward that occurs than to become paralysed with superstitious emotionalism and be helplessly swayed by influences which might otherwise be either ignored or put to good account.

There is no Black Magic, however powerful, no evil force nor astral horror which can have the slightest effect upon anyone who does not contain a strain of the same vibration in their own make-up. One who is completely honest and whole-heartedly trusts in the power of good is an untouchable as far as evil influences are concerned. 'According to thy faith be it done unto thee.'

Therefore when any evil influences or threats of misfortune approach, the one attacked needs only to cleanse his own heart of fear, doubt or any ulterior motives, and he is at once protected by his own vibrations. If we tune our wireless in to Paris we do not get Moscow, and if we tune our personal wireless in to good fortune all other vibrations will flow through and onwards without finding any anchorage. It is upon this principle that the Christian Scientists and many others work. They know that the fear of anything is a very powerful magnet which draws that thing inevitably to the fearful one. As Job said, 'That which I greatly feared has come upon me.'

Fear, laziness and lack of sincerity are therefore the defects which will lead the seeker on to the 'left-hand path' instead of the 'right-hand path'. The natural Karma of this is that he will have to do twice the work before he finally reaches his true goal.

But if a sharp lookout is kept for the various pitfalls and illusions pointed out in this chapter much waste of time and many painful humiliations may be avoided.

Remember that it is always possible to go straight to the innermost goal and ignore the various stratas of comparatively petty psychic and mental phenomena which lie in between. The really wise have learnt to *know*. They want neither proof nor practice, and they enjoy bliss and glory here and now, in spite of all circumstances and irrespective of either past, present or future.

19

THE SUMMING-UP

AN EFFORT has been made in this book to take a necessarily summarized survey of life as it confronts the independent seeker. The existence of a vast accumulation of so-called knowledge and belief has been pointed out. The conceptions of the cosmos which have held sway over millions for thousands of years have been briefly sketched.

There remains one final theory to be expounded—that which is called by some people 'Epigenisis'.

The name means 'an addition to that which was created', in other words Evolution or Progress. It concerns itself with the fact that in the continual reincarnation of all particles and phases of life the memory of experience is brought back *plus* the deductions and adaptation gained from that experience. The evolution of plant, insect, animal, man and planet consists of a gradual refining, strengthening and perfecting under the ever-changing influences of still greater developing bodies. Even in the vast cycles of historical development each recurring sequence of Golden Age, Dark Age and Age of Energy is reproduced on a higher and more powerful note, and embraces the tackling of more difficult conditions.

Humanity has just been required to pass through an age of deeper ignorance, a more profound Blind Spot, than ever before, and has passed through it creditably. It may therefore look forward to a Golden Age which will bring deeper fulfilment and wider understanding and power than any preceding.

Epigenisis is the answer to those who say that the world has not progressed, but only if they are ready energetically to seek this answer for themselves. In studying the great religions of the world, therefore, Epigenisis must be taken into account.

Each of the great Teachers of the world, Zoroaster, Krishna, Lao Tze, Buddha, adapted former teachings to the future needs of developing humanity, even though humanity lagged far behind in taking advantage of it. Therefore it is to the last great Teacher, Jesus Christ, that we must look for the most advanced ideal and the latest message to humanity. We find that His work was to transfer the possibility of attainment from the few to the many, to simplify the great Truths for the use of all humanity and to introduce the ultimate act of attainment, the awakening of the Love principle in the heart, to mankind. His teaching has been in some ways too simple for muddled and inhibited generations to grasp, but after 2000 years there are faint signs that the seed sown is about to burst into life.

Now, leaving the religious aspect completely on one side, let us consider entirely from the scientific point of view what the great teachings of the world, headed by Jesus Christ's, would do for humanity if put into practise.

The medical profession agrees that human beings are prey to the act of auto-intoxication, that is so say that they flood their own systems with various poisons bred by various states of the mind and emotions. The most poisonous of these states are fear, anger, worry, sentimental emotionalism and envy. The destructive emanations set up by these mental and emotional states must be clogging the virility and sensitivity of the race like a heavy pall, and we should not forget to add the emanations from terrified slaughtered animals to the general agglomeration.

This terrible pall of thought-poison is of course the breeding-place for all those 'instincts' which make war, murder, cruelty, lust and stupidity possible. It beats with a heavy vibration, to which people are drawn, as a speck of iron is drawn to a magnet, if they have no stronger vibration of their own. From a scientific point of view their only protection is to develop stronger vibrations, which are those of love, hope, belief, charity, idealism and intellect—in other words, to learn actually to 'love one's neighbour as oneself' and to 'have faith even as a grain of mustard-seed'.

The result therefore of everyone obeying these plain injunctions would be to overpower, melt or short-circuit this heavy pall, this rubbish-heap of bad thoughts, breeding-spot for the microbes of mental disease.

Universal love, as we have pointed out, produces an understanding of all that exists in nature.

The result of faith would be a lack of self-poisoning and therefore perfect health.

The result of idealism and intellectual development would be complete normality of the reproductive functions, which would produce in its turn perfect eugenic conditions and a natural birth-control. And the highly increased mental capacity thus evoked would be available for the solving of those economic and social problems which defeat the people of today.

The practice of meditation, deep breathing and self-analysis can certainly be the means of pulling people out of the Slough of Despond of accumulated generations of bad habits. It constitutes a scientific process of short-circuiting undesirable vibrations.

From the purely scientific point of view therefore the following of the rules set forth by the great Teachers would speedily produce ideal world conditions and the hygienic, eugenic superman for which some nations are already striving, however imperfectly.

From that which is called the 'spiritual' point of view, however, the prospect is infinitely more thrilling, inspiring and illuminating. He who is drawn to spiritual endeavour, who feels the call and the pull of the inner mysteries, will embark on a pilgrimage in which there is no turning back. He will go through the stages of studying the self, developing the self, and then forgetting the self completely. He will then realize that the ultimate privilege and joy, as Jesus Christ came to show, is to serve.

His battle-cry will be 'Service'. At first he will rush around trying to serve, and getting very much in the way of his own inspiration. Later he will realize that true service is first of all to 'Be'. He will understand that if he has once polarized himself to be a permanent channel or 'receiving station' for the Light of Wisdom, and can hold himself in that state of constant and unchanging radiation, he can become a fixed power-house, a torch in the realms of the mind. He can link up with others on the higher levels of their super-conscious, he can speak to them and teach them in that sphere where are no words, flooding them with illumination, peace and faith from his own storehouse. They have merely to think of his name and at once feel the anchorage of his vibrations.

He learns finally how not to make conscious 'effort' to help others, how not to interfere with their lives or their own way of working out their salvation. He learns not to criticize but to understand, and to be able to interpret them to themselves if they ask it, so that they can learn the particular lessons and reason of their difficulties. He learns to speak to each one who comes to him in his own language and on his own level; he learns to leave in peace those who do not seek his help, and to be a power of ready quiet strength to those who do.

Such an aspirant will begin by envisaging the Path before him, the progress from student to Probationer, from Probationer to Disciple, from Disciple to Initiate, from Initiate to Master, from Master to Lord of a Planet and so on upwards and onwards illimitably. The dazzling prospect will spur him on over the difficult drudgery of the early steps.

But when the gate of his heart is finally opened and the mystery of Love floods his being, then all thoughts of his own progress are obliterated, and he would gratefully stay behind until the last faulty little pilgrim has passed safely on before him.

He waits and watches and helps, and suddenly he finds that he is one in activity and in mind with the Creator Himself. These things, however, cannot be expressed in words, although much glorious poetry and philosophy have been poured out in the effort.

All through history humanity has been offered the Key of Heaven, even as this little book attempts to offer it.

Men exist as partially dead creatures until they have used this key and opened their hearts and minds to Reality. Then they are flooded with such life and brilliance and illumination that they do indeed experience a 'second birth' infinitely greater than the first.

As a final word, then, the value of the information touched upon in this book is merely that it can provide the reader with a tool for the building of his life. Like a knife, which can be used either to murder a beautiful life or to carve out an everlasting work of art, the value of the tool depends upon the user. It can quite definitely be used for unimagined achievement if the motive-power be sincerity and the highest aspiration.

Or it can result in a conceited boast of superior knowledge, the act of the 'big fish in the little pond', if the ideals are not sufficiently strong.

Or again it can fall to the ground through lazy inattention.

It is for each individual reader to decide whether he wishes to become a vital force for good, and to realize that until he is truly living for the world and not for himself he will never achieve anything of that which is thrilling, joyful, wonderful and inspiring.

A selfish person is short-circuited; nothing from outside can flow through.

Some people are not selfish, however, but self-centred, which is just as inhibiting. They are kind, generous and vivacious at times, but their thoughts revolve round their own kindness and all their little personal affairs unceasingly, how *they* feel and felt, what others think of *them*, what *they* know, how *they* love, what *they* must do, how *they* must help. They are complete prisoners inside their own little personality. It is this 'I' 'I' attitude which is so very difficult to get over, and which is such a subtle handicap to many.

The only importance the personality has is that it is there as a sort of buffer, to teach one how completely to get the better of it! PERSONALITY VERSUS INDIVIDUALITY! How can we discriminate between these two? The difference is much the same as between emotion and love. Individuality, the real thing, is a calm, steady, deep and lasting force felt within a person—his essence, that which composes the ego or inner man.

Personality (the word comes from *persona*, meaning mask) comprises all the little surface peculiarities, moods and changes, all which has to do with physical life, disturbing, evanescent and unimportant. In astrology individuality is that unchanging part of us governed by the sun, while the moon rules the unstable personality.

In true sacrifice and service we use our individuality and keep our personality in complete abeyance. This is what is called slaying our lower man or killing the dragon!

TRUE LIVING. If we can learn to love, think and serve as above described, the mind will become so powerful and co-ordinated, that it will unerringly direct all other of our activities.

Our calm enthusiasm will inevitably give us that slow, deep and powerful breathing which will finally become automatic with us.

But if we start at the wrong end by an intensive training in breathing it may give us animal health, it may upset our nervous system, it may even put us in a madhouse, but it certainly will not give us a ready-made loving heart or wise and potent mind.

By the same token, with a mind and heart awake we will instinctively know how, when and what to eat. Our calmness will give us that slowness and sparingness in eating which is the first neglected essential, and our continual development will go hand in hand with a continual modification and change in our diet.

But if we begin at the wrong end by becoming diet cranks we may improve our bodies or we may ruin them—the chances are pretty equal, but we will no more create a ready-made wisdom and power that way than by breathing.

If our hearts and minds are rightly orientated we will quite naturally be drawn to those few studies and people with whom we can further our particular work—our choice will be unerring and inspired.

But if we start at the other end with absorption in theoretical studies, teachers and cults, and count on such outside help for our progress, and have not a strictly honest desire for the truth alone, we shall fall into any number of traps, and meet with danger and disillusionment and misery. The false always apes the real. It is only true honesty in ourselves which acts as a tuning-fork to recognize honesty in another.

Many people are drawn to the Great Search through a feeling

of loneliness—that wistful misunderstood loneliness which attacks them in the midst of friends and festivities, and which is really the longing of the soul for unity in service with those who *know*, and for the realization that they are part of a wonderful whole—that they belong and are essential to a glorious plan. Loneliness also comes from being self-centred instead of world-centred, from a craving for a personal love and reward, and thereby the imprisoning of oneself in a tiny mental compartment.

Service leads finally to working with others, the beginning of that Universal Brotherhood which some of us cannot yet picture, yet which is inevitably and actually coming into being before our eyes.

The various banners of the vanguard of this Universal Brotherhood are already flinging a challenge right across the world. To anyone who wishes to achieve fulfilment for himself and to help to build the future Golden Age, the way is now wide open. The beginning has been made, the world is passing rapidly from Dark Age into Light, and there remain now only the fetters of man's own blindness or laziness to hold him back. Let us shake off these fetters and move forward with those happy ones who are achieving their birthright—the triumph of Godhood in human form.

The author would be glad to hear from readers who are interested in the subject of human evolution and world progress.

BIBLIOGRAPHY

The Secret Doctrine, by H. P. Blavatsky.

The Rosicrucian Cosmo-Conception, by Max Heindel.

From Intellect to Intuition, by Alice A. Bailey.

The Zodiac and the Salts of Salvation, by Dr. George W. Carey and Inez Eudora Perry.

The Secret Path, by Paul Brunton.

The Story of Oriental Philosophy, by L. Adams Beck.

The Secret of the Golden Flower, by Wilhelm and Jung.

The Detection of Disease, by Oscar Parkes and Eric Perkins.

The Garden of Vision, by L. Adams Beck.

Akhnaton, by Arthur Weigall.

Ancient Egypt the Light of the World, by Gerald Massey.

Initiation Human and Solar, by Alice A. Bailey.

Your Mysterious Glands, by H. H. Rubin, M.D.

Works on Colour, by Dr. Babbitt, from his *The Principles of Light and Colour*.

Your Days are Numbered, by Florence Campbell.

Light and Colours, by Colville.

Practical Numerology, by C. G. Sander.

The Problem of Atlantis, by Lewis Spence.